"A praisesong delivered in the authentic and loving voice of a sister who clearly cherishes Black women. Julia Boyd gives us a shoulder to lean on, a hand to hold, a smile to fall into, and a raised eyebrow to bring us back to our senses and help us remember how wonderful we are."
—Evelyn C. White, editor,
The Black Women's Health Book:

"This book radiates   that has
never been done be   nphs,
and disappointments   ewing
my own spirit."   esident,
                              ....ms Agency

"An explosive message for women . . . an insightful and witty guide to elevating one's pride in self."
—King Features Syndicate

"Through her wise advice Boyd brings warmth, humor, and common sense to all her sisters who struggle each day for self-esteem." —*Oakland Tribune*

"It makes such good sense to write a book addressed specifically to Black women that one wonders why it hasn't been done more often in the past." —*Milwaukee Journal*

"A timely piece of work." —*Des Moines Sunday Register*

"The first of its kind to speak specifically to Black women about mental health." —*Seattle Times*

"Not only do African-American women need to absorb these messages themselves; they need to imbue their children with a sense of self-worth." —*New York Daily News*

"A sassy self-help book that brings a message of rebirth and renewal." —*St. Louis American*

JULIA A. BOYD is a psychotherapist practicing in Seattle, Washington. She lectures widely, and her short fiction has appeared in several small-press anthologies and in *Essence* magazine.

ALSO BY JULIA A. BOYD

*Girlfriend to Girlfriend: Everyday Wisdom
and Affirmations from the Sister Circle*

*Embracing the Fire: Sisters Talk About Sex
and Relationships*

IN THE
COMPANY
OF MY
SISTERS

BLACK WOMEN
AND SELF-ESTEEM

▼▲▼▲▼▲▼▲▼▲▼▲▼▲▼

JULIA A. BOYD

A PLUME BOOK

For my grandmothers
Annie Dunn 1904–
Julia Conyers 1901–1941

PLUME
Published by the Penguin Group
Penguin Books USA Inc., 375 Hudson Street, New York, New York 10014, U.S.A.
Penguin Books Ltd, 27 Wrights Lane, London W8 5TZ, England
Penguin Books Australia Ltd, Ringwood, Victoria, Australia
Penguin Books Canada Ltd, 10 Alcorn Avenue, Toronto, Ontario, Canada M4V 3B2
Penguin Books (N.Z.) Ltd, 182–190 Wairau Road, Auckland 10, New Zealand

Penguin Books Ltd, Registered Offices: Harmondsworth, Middlesex, England

Published by Plume, an imprint of Dutton Signet,
a division of Penguin Books USA Inc.
Previously published in a Dutton edition.

First Plume Printing, February, 1997
10 9 8 7 6 5 4 3 2 1

"Ancient Places" copyright © 1993 by Charlotte Watson Sherman.
"Transformation" by Julia Boyd, was first published in *Poetic Liberties*.

 REGISTERED TRADEMARK—MARCA REGISTRADA

The Library of Congress has catalogued the Dutton edition as follows:
Boyd, Julia A. Conyers.
    In the company of my sisters: Black women and self-esteem/Julia A. Conyers
Boyd.
        p.   cm.
    ISBN 0-525-93708-0 (hc.)
    ISBN 0-452-27246-7 (pbk.)
    1. Afro-American women—Life skills guides.   2. Afro-American
women—Psychology.   I. Title.
E185.86.B648   1993
305.48'896073—dc20   93–17163
                                                  CIP

Printed in the United States of America
Original hardcover design by Leonard Telesca

Acknowledgments

Special journeys are rarely made alone, and Lord knows I've had a lot of help. So I want to give a heartfelt thanks to all of my traveling companions. To Elizabeth Wales, my agent, for believing in me and the strength of my work. To Carole DeSanti, my editor, for seeing my vision and helping it become a reality. Thanks to Deborah Berger for helping me to dot my *i*'s and cross my *t*'s.

To my family: my parents, Joseph and Lavada Conyers; my sisters, Wilda Fulton, Barbara Cook, Geneva Wyatt, Rose Conyers, and Lavada Lester; and my brothers, Joseph, Dennis, and Anthony Conyers; your continued love and support gave me the courage to keep going during the hard times.

To my sister circle: Colleen McElroy, Jody Kim, Nancy Rawls, Marsha Leslie, Marilyn Fullen-Collins, Raina Shields, and Alma Arnold; your love and support held me up when I fell down. To Charlotte "Write-it-down-cause-I-need-to-read-it" Watson Sherman for her steady and unwavering support. Carletta "Girlfriend" Wilson, who kept me on track during the rough times. Special thanks to Doris Harris, my late-night telephone buddy; your calm feedback and encouragement worked miracles on my shattered nerves. To my partner in shopping madness, Gail Myers. To Lyn Simkins; you held the mirror in which I saw myself—thank you. Rick Simonson of Elliott Bay Books and his lovely wife, Barbara; it's really party time now. To the gang at Red and Black Books; you're great. To the women at "Tess" for always helping me to look my very best. To my very special friend Terry Nilsen, for always being here, there, and everywhere for me. And last but not least, the biggest thanks goes to my son, Michael, for being the star in my life; and to my other child, Raymond Hayes, thanks for being the brother Michael never had.

Contents

PART THREE

▼▲▼▲▼▲▼

LORD, HOLD MY HAND
WHILE I RUN THIS RACE

PART FOUR

▼▲▼▲▼▲▼

PUBLIC LIES AND PRIVATE TRUTHS

PART FIVE

▼▲▼▲▼▲▼

IN THE COMPANY OF MY SISTERS

Introduction

No Images
She does not know her beauty
She thinks her brown body
has no glory
But if she could dance naked
'neath palm trees
& see her reflection in the river
then she would know
but there are no trees
on the street
where she lives
& dishwater gives back
no images
—Waring Cuney

When I was five years old, my mother thought I was having an identity crisis because I wanted a Toni Home Permanent for Little Girls. Actually, Momi's reaction was quite innocent now that I think about it. I was sitting crouched down between her legs as she was combing my hair. In order to keep me still through the tedious process of parting, greasing, and braiding, she had the television set tuned to my favorite cartoon show. With Momi brushing and combing, I was as engrossed in the program as any five-year-old can be. Then, lo and behold, a commercial came on showing this angelic little white girl crying as her mother tries to comb her long, tangled, wet hair; then, all of a sudden, her mom gets the bright idea to use a Toni Home Permanent for Little Girls. The next shot shows the mother removing the last curler and the little angel smiling sweetly at her mother, thanking her for the beautiful, bouncy tangle-free curls. End of commercial.

"Well," my five-year-old logic reasoned, "if it works for her, why not for me?" So I told Momi I wanted a Toni. Without missing a stroke, Momi replied in her best Momi voice, "Baby, what did you notice about that little girl?" Ah! a trick question for sure, but I was ready with my speedy five-year-old answer: "She was on T.V. and she didn't cry anymore at the end." I'm sure my mother smiled at my answer. I couldn't see her smile, but I'm sure I heard it in her voice, as she continued combing. "Baby, that little girl was white" (as if to explain the obvious difference that my little eyes had missed). But being unconcerned with the little girl's physical coloring, I assumed that Momi had missed the point. I didn't care what color she was. I wanted tangle-free hair, so I responded in the only way I knew how, which was "Momi, I don't want the lil girl, I want a Toni." Momi, continuing to be patient, but becoming more firm, then explained that little white girls had different hair than little Negro (we hadn't become "Black" yet) girls. The underlying message was "Pay attention, there's a lesson to be learned here."

This childhood reflection stands out for me because it's the first time I can honestly pinpoint being told by one of my parents that I was in fact different from others. It's also the first time I can truly remember starting to notice ethnic differences between myself and others.

I grew up in Parkside, a then solidly middle-class subdivision of Camden, New Jersey. My neighborhood was multicultural, and I had a pretty liberal dose of Italian, Jewish, and Black friends. But my playmates at that time were all little girls within my age group. Our biggest issue at the age of five wasn't the fact that Sally was Jewish (and white) or that Angie was Italian (and white) or that Jackie and Sharon were Black; our biggest problem was who was going turn and who was going to jump rope first in our daily game of double-dutch. Sure, Sally and Angie had long hair that flopped around when they jumped, and Jackie's, Sharon's, and my hair didn't flop. But it never really occurred to me that their hair flopped because they were white—that is, until Momi pointed it out to me.

Maybe as a five-year-old Black girl I was naive to ethnic, cultural, and color differences. But it just didn't seem to matter all that much to me or my friends. Momi didn't realize it at the time (or maybe she did), but her sixty-second lesson on the differences between white and Black hair became the first in a series of lifelong lessons about being a Black woman in American society.

There's a commonly held, radical belief among many Blacks that as Blacks we've been stripped of our identity. I believe that as Black women our personal and collective identities have been at best hidden, and at worst warped beyond recognition by the unrelenting negative messages we get from society at large. For many years, the only media images I saw of Black women came from *Ebony* or *Jet* magazine. Even at that time, as at the present, the images rarely showed us as we really are: diverse individuals who don't fit into neat little boxes. Even more basically, if we are to believe the commercial media, the voice of America, it's been just within the past ten years that Blacks have used toothpaste, aspirin, deodorant, or chewing gum, or eaten at McDonald's.

However, as Black women we're a creative, stubborn group, and while society has repeatedly given us negative messages, we've refused to listen. Let's hear it for being hardheaded!

We have started re-creating our image bit by bit and piece by piece, thumbing our noses at Mr. Society. In fact, we are so good at our own recreation that Mr. Society has started to imitate us: Bo Derek's cornrows, Barbara Hershey's full lips, and Coppertone skin. The difficulty lies in having to constantly justify and defend our individuality—as Black women, a group that has long been ignored or dismissed.

Here, *In the Company of My Sisters*, I share my search

for identity, understanding, and strength, with the purpose of helping myself and my sisters achieve a stronger and healthier sense of self-esteem in a world that can definitely get you down. I'm also sharing something else—a fabulous group of Black women without whom this book would not have been written.

Every month I meet with a group of very talented and beautiful sisters. We shoot the breeze, eat mass quantities of food, brag on ourselves and each other, and talk about everything from the political to the personal. Over the years, I've come to regard this group of women—plus a few precious others—as my family, my sister circle. We've shared major triumphs and traumatic events together: there's never a question of needing or getting emotional support because we all know that support is only a telephone call away. These women are my family of choice. We chose each other based on our adult needs for friendship, closeness, and community. As in any family, we're not all the same, but that's what makes us good together. What bonds us is our ability to trust and respect each other as individuals.

Because of issues of privacy, I can't introduce you to each of the sisters personally. The names and personal identities of these sisters have been changed; however, the issues, questions, and feedback they present are very real.

So pull up a chair, take a load off, and join us, as we celebrate who we are and who we are becoming in the company of our sisters.

PART ONE

▼△▼△▼△▼△▼

IS THIS A BLACK THING?

I

▼▲▼▲▼

What Is Self-Esteem?

When I was growing up in Camden, New Jersey, my favorite pastime was reading. I was sick with eczema much of the time, and to escape the curious and hurtful taunts of other children, I buried myself in books. Books allowed me the pleasure of retreating into a world where I was healthy, strong, and capable of doing anything. Curled up in my favorite armchair, I became a heroine who mastered all challenges, winning my right to a fulfilled life. Closest to my heart and my imagination were stories in which women challenged adversity and won.

I adored *Gone with the Wind.* That Miz Scarlett was my kind of woman: she took on the good, bad, and ugly with equal strength and determination; that girl didn't take no stuff. Yes, ma'am, I was Miz Scarlett. Curled up in that big gray armchair, I became Scarlett, the saucy mistress who teased and flirted with captivating suitors. In my ten-year-old imagination, I was the Scarlett who lusted after Ashley Wilkes, won Rhett Butler's heart, and saved the family plantation, Tara. Knowing how fond I was of this particular book, my mother decided to give me a special treat, and she took me to see the movie. As soon as the opening credits ended, my excitement turned to complete shock and disappointment when the very white-skinned Vivien Leigh answered to the name "Scarlett."

Sitting in the theater, I was trying to figure out what was wrong with this picture. When Hattie McDaniel stuck her handkerchief-wrapped head out of the window to call "Miss Scarlett" into the house, I got the message loud and clear. Obviously my imagination had distorted some critical literary information regarding the who's who of *Gone with the Wind*.

As I grew older, I realized that images of Black women as heroines were absent from the pages of my books, thereby placing some constraints on my imaginative powers of seeing myself as a confident and powerful Black woman.

As an adult, I've often asked myself if this childhood incident had any effect on my sense of self-esteem. The answer is yes, because this one incident gave me a personal message that changed into a personal belief. But before I reveal more about my personal belief, let's take a look at self-esteem and how we develop this sense of ourselves.

Self-esteem is a core of personal beliefs that we develop about ourselves over the years. We receive many of these core beliefs from messages that are directed at us, both individually and collectively, as Black women. We're not always conscious of taking in the messages, but if we're repeatedly exposed to the same message, we begin to internalize the messages, which then become beliefs. We unconsciously store these beliefs away until a situation or event occurs that pushes that hidden message into our current reality. For example, if every time you make a decision someone tells you that you're stupid, you're going to turn that message into a hidden belief. And when a situation arises that calls for you to make a decision, the hidden message that you've received will present itself: "I can't make decisions, I'm stupid." You'll be left feeling confused and frustrated.

Self-esteem is a universal concept. I believe that all God's children are born with healthy self-esteem—I've never come across a baby who hated herself. However, all God's children aren't treated or perceived as being universally equal (as I discovered vis-à-vis MGM), so therefore the degree to which we experience self-esteem is going to be universally different.

To develop and maintain a healthy sense of self-esteem, we need to receive two basic messages—"I am lovable, and I am worthwhile"—and we need to get these messages consistently. While these two messages seem fairly clear and direct, the reality is that they are very complex. The complexity is not in the words, but in our belief in the words. It's easy to say, "I am lovable and worthwhile," but much more difficult for us to believe it.

It takes three things to turn a message into a belief:

1. **The message must be given in a clear, direct manner.**
2. **There has to be supportive evidence that increases the validity of the message.**
3. **The message must be repeated over an extended period of time.**

Although we're born with healthy self-esteem, as we grow from childhood to adulthood, we receive countless messages that overshadow and diminish our early beliefs in our worth. As Black women, we have been the recipients of many distorted messages about our ethnicity and our femaleness. These distorted messages are repeatedly reinforced through the media, in our personal contacts, sometimes even in our families. When we internalize these messages, they cloud and poison our self-esteem. It's like eating bad food or breathing toxic air—we get sick.

Having a healthy sense of self-esteem means reexamining our current personal belief system and tossing out those beliefs and messages that produce thoughts and feelings of self-doubt.

Like most things in our lives, our self-esteem operates on a continuum that includes highs, lows, and in-betweens. But, you guessed it, that continuum is affected by the messages we give ourselves. So on days when all is right with the world, more than likely we'll feel okay— that is, if we pay attention to how we feel. On days when we feel that the whole world is going to hell in a handbasket, and we need to blame ourselves, we'll feel like s——, and on days when we believe we've saved the world, we'll feel good about ourselves.

As for me, reading *Gone with the Wind* allowed me to believe I was Scarlett, with all of her lovable charm. Seeing the movie *Gone with the Wind* zapped me back into the "Black reality" of being a small, powerless ten-year-old Black girl child. Could I still be lovable if I wasn't white? The personal message I gave myself was yes! I tossed out the idea of being the woman on the silver screen, but I kept the belief that I could have her larger-than-life characteristics of spunkiness, persistence, and courage.

Remember, girlfriend, the equation looks like this: **clear direct message + supportive evidence + repetition = personal belief (self-esteem).**

2

▼▲▼▲▼

Something's Got a Hold on Me

> If you want a thing to be
> take your time go slowly
> do one thing
> and do it well
> simple things are holy.

It seems like a hundred years ago now, but really it was
only about ten, and I can't remember where I heard it, but
this simple little saying literally saved my life. I had just
started graduate school and to top it off I was in the midst
of an ugly marital separation that ultimately ended in divorce. I believed that my life was over; after all, having
been raised as a dyed-in-the-wool Catholic, I just knew
that marriage was forever. Even worse, I envisioned myself as contributing to the often-cited statistic of the growing numbers of unmarried Black females. I could just see
the headlines: NEWS FLASH: ANOTHER SINGLE BLACK FEMALE
PARENT ADDS TO NATIONAL CRISIS. I was just crushed. My
mental and emotional state was so low that I'm sure I
alone raised the status of clinical depression to an art
form.

And I was scared to death. Here I was with a young son
dependent on me for his survival, and the biggest decisions I had ever made amounted to whether I should buy
high heels or flats and what color. So we're talking about
this girlfriend being a major mess. I needed help and I
needed it fast. Family and friends were encouraging, but
much too close to my emotional pain to be objective. I

wanted help, they wanted me to be strong. As much as I tried to follow everyone's well-intended advice, my attempts to be strong led only to frequent trips to the local emergency room for treatment of recurring severe outbreaks of eczema and acute asthma. After my third trip to the E.R. with my usual complaints—"I need to breathe so I can scratch my itch"—my physician, in his calm, nonintrusive manner, suggested that I might want to discuss my problems with a therapist. Now I knew I needed help, and trying to decide whether to scratch or breathe gave me a clue that something was physically wrong, but clearly this man suspected that I needed more than ointment and pills to cure what ailed me. I was depressed, scared, desperate, itching, and short of breath—what did I have to lose?

The therapist I selected came highly recommended; she was as calm and patient as I was anxious and fearful. To my unending questions, she had but one response:

"You will survive this crisis over time, and along the way you'll learn many new things about yourself."

"What will I learn?" I wanted to know.

"How to take care of yourself."

"How can I do that?"

"By taking one thing at a time, and going slowly," she calmly replied.

It was after this first session that I heard the saying that begins this chapter. Thus began my journey to healthy self-esteem.

So often our sense of self-esteem is based on our ability to please someone else: family, friends, lovers, employers, and the like. When one of these relationships breaks, we believe, as I had in the case of my divorce, that we've failed our given mission in life, as *strong Black women*.

The view we have of ourselves is often deeply rooted in the internalized personal messages we give ourselves on a daily basis over long periods of time. Sometimes we give ourselves positive messages—"I'm a beautiful Black woman"—but generally our personal messages are negative—"I'm a failure." And as if we weren't hard enough on ourselves privately, as Black women our internalized personal messages have over the years been continually infused with negative myths and stereotypes that unconsciously feed into how we view ourselves.

In *Black Macho and the Myth of the Superwoman* (Routledge, New York: Chapman & Hall, 1990), author Michele Wallace presents the following long-standing stereotypes and myths that we as Black women have received as messages over the years:

Sapphire. Mammy. Tragic mulatto wench. Workhorse, can swing an ax, lift a load, pick cotton with any man. A wonderful housekeeper. Excellent with children. Very clean. Very religious. A terrific mother. A great singer and dancer and a devoted teacher and social worker. She's always had more opportunities than the black man because she was no threat to the white man so he made it easy for her. But curiously enough, she frequently ends up on welfare. Nevertheless, she is more educated and makes more money than the black man. She is more likely to be employed and more likely to be a professional than the black man. And subsequently she provides the main support for the family. Not beautiful, rather hard looking unless she has white blood, but then very beautiful. The black ones are exotic though, great in bed, tigers, and very fertile. If she is middle class she tends to be uptight about sex, prudish. She is hard on and unsupportive of black men, domineering, castrating. She tends to wear the pants around her house. Very strong. Sorrow rolls right off her brow like so much rain. Tough. Unfeminine, opposed to women's rights movements, considers herself already liberated. Nevertheless unworldly. Definitely not a dreamer, rigid, inflexible, uncompassionate, lacking in goals any more imaginative than a basket of fried chicken and a good fuck.

While on the surface, we can deny that these messages have any real effect on us, the bottom line is that we can't help but be influenced on some unconscious level, because these distorted messages have been systematically repeated and illustrated over and over again through songs, movies, television, and books throughout the years.

Della, a thirty-nine-year-old, married office worker with a fourteen-year-old daughter and fifteen-year-old son, expresses a very real example of just how these negative myths and stereotypes continue to stay alive even in our own communities.

> *I was listening to one of those rap songs the other day, and all through the song the group kept referring to the women as bitches and whores. I was really offended, but when I said something to my fourteen-year-old daughter about the lyrics, she told me I was old-fashioned and being too sensitive. "After all," she said, "it's only a song." How can I expect my daughter to have any self-respect when she hears young Black men refer to Black women as bitches and whores?*

This is but one example of how we start receiving messages that devalue our self-worth as women. After hearing these messages over a period of time, we not only devalue ourselves but other Black women too.

For example, during the controversy surrounding the Clarence Thomas–Anita Hill hearings, it was evident that many of our Black sisters condemned Professor Hill for telling her truth about Judge Thomas's sexual harassment. These sisters based their condemnations on their personal core beliefs that are in some way tied to the myth that Black women are unsupportive of Black men.

It was also clear to me that, through their own experiences of abuse, a large number of our sisters identified very strongly with Professor Hill's pain. While the first group of sisters has been very vocal in their disapproval of

Professor Hill, the second group of sisters has been almost silent.

When I asked one sister in my practice about her noticeable long-time silence concerning the sexual harassment she suffered for years from a coworker, she pointedly replied, "Well, when the president of the United States gets on national television and discounts the credibility of an educated professional Black sister like Anita Hill, what chance do I have that someone is going to believe me?" So, you can see, the cycle continues.

It's so true that when we fail to hold ourselves accountable, we lack the courage to hold others accountable. We've become so accustomed to the distorted messages given to us by others that it's become almost acceptable to hold ourselves, as well as other Black women, hostage by continuing to believe and repeat those messages that are meant to offend and hurt us. As Black women, we have to work harder to dispel the myths and stereotypes that plague our image.

Several years ago, I was sitting in my dermatologist's office for what seemed like the umpteenth time in as many weeks (I had just finalized my divorce). I wanted the good doctor to work his medical magic on my skin, because I believed at that time that unmarked skin equaled beautiful Black woman. And I was determined to be beautiful and my blasted eczema was getting in the way. While bemoaning my fate, I started flipping through an old copy of a women's magazine, and I noticed an article by Marcia Ann Gillespie, a well-known Black female journalist. As I scanned her article on personal acceptance (believe me, there are no mistakes in the universe), I found myself reversing my former beliefs about beauty. In her article Ms. Gillespie apologized to all the sisters she had ever hurt because of her own lack of self-acceptance, which began with an incident from her childhood. It appears that someone had made a cruel remark about how she looked as a child. For many years, this remark, "You have an old hard cold face," shadowed Ms. Gillespie's personal acceptance and her acceptance of other Black women. As she grew older and wiser, Ms. Gillespie was able to recognize the cruel remark for what it was—an attempt to hurt her. After growing to the point where she was able to define and accept a sense of beauty that included her imperfections, Ms. Gillespie was able to extend her sense of beauty to other Black women. To paraphrase, Ms. Gillespie stated that if she recognizes another Black woman's beauty, it is only because she has learned to accept her own beauty with all of her imperfections.

This one sentence hit me like a ton of bricks. Here I was sacrificing my sense of self because of the distorted concept that having perfect skin would make me more beautiful—but beautiful to whom? I had forgotten somewhere along the way that my skin condition wasn't a reflection of my identity as a Black woman. Thanks to this article, I could suspend for a time my personal belief that I wasn't beautiful because of my skin condition.

In this personal reflection and the one about my divorce, it's clear that I had internalized the personal message that I was a failure if my life wasn't perfect according to someone else's standards. By examining my personal internalized messages slowly, one at a time, I learned how to replace my poor self-esteem messages with more powerful realistic messages.

Here's a simple exercise that will help you to get in touch with your negative, internalized personal messages. Let's face it, girlfriend, you can't change the messages without knowing what they are. This exercise will help you to replace the negative stuff with something more positive. Now first of all I want to let you in on a little secret. These messages tend to be quick, and because they're in your head, no one else can hear them but you. We're talking about paying close attention to what you say to yourself. Another tip on recognizing the messages is that they often have certain words attached to them, words such as *should,* as in "I should have . . . ," or *never,* as in "I never . . . ," or *always,* as in "I always . . ." Get the picture?

Now for the exercise. Every time you give yourself a negative message, snap your finger. Not a loud partying finger-pop snap, just a gentle snap. For each snap make a mark on a sheet of paper. At the end of the day, count up the number of marks on your paper. If you can remember what you told yourself, write it down. Look at what you told yourself, and see if you can come up with a more realistic message.

Example: I must be a failure or I wouldn't be getting a divorce.
More realistic message: Being divorced doesn't make me a failure as a woman. I'm still a good person.

Example: I should get off welfare and find a decent job.
More realistic message: I don't like being on welfare, but finding a job would be hard because I don't have employment skills. I can talk to my caseworker about taking some classes to help me get on my feet.

Example: I'll never be pretty, 'cause I'm too fat.
More realistic message: I don't like being this heavy, but I'm still an attractive woman. I can talk to my doctor about losing some weight.

Don't be discouraged if the messages don't change right away—you didn't learn these negative messages overnight. Just remember:

> If you want a thing to be
> take your time go slowly
> do one thing
> and do it well
> simple things are holy.

3

▼▲▼▲▼

What Makes Self-Esteem
Different for Us?

Transformation
In Loree's beauty shop
hot combs sizzled
against
wet oily scalps
branding
grown woman fantasies
into tender young
heads.
Thick bushy afros
became
long glossy black curls
transforming
natural Black queens
into
commercial mahogany princesses.

My aunt Loree was a prominent beautician in Camden. I can still hear her words as I sat, at age ten, tall and proud in her chair: "When I'm through with you, you're going to look like a little princess." Since I had read numerous fairy tales but had never come across a Black princess, I was expecting to be transformed into Snow White, seven little men and all, the moment my aunt uttered the magic words "I'm done." But when she handed me the mirror and all I saw was my face framed with shiny black curls, I just couldn't hold back the tears.

I'm sure that my aunt was truly baffled by my response, but how could I explain that her magical powers to transform were way off-base? Aunt Loree, if you're looking down, I'm sorry. I was ten and didn't know you were talk'n about making me a *Black* princess.

My aunt's message was well intended, but as well-intended messages often do, it got lost in translation. Having a healthy sense of self-esteem is sometimes difficult for us as Black women because we have to sift continuously through the well-intended messages in order to get to the underlying content.

Well, I'm Nettie and I'm thirty-four years old. I've been with my boyfriend, Fred, for three years and I don't have any kids. I work as a legal secretary downtown. Anyway, I was going to say that I really hear what you're say'n about being told I'm a strong Black woman. I swear if one more person tells me what a strong Black woman I am, I'm go'n make like Sampson and tear them apart. I know they mean well, but the truth is I'm no stronger than the next person, and hearing that all the time makes me feel bad, 'cause try'n to live up to it is wearing me out.

We can all relate to that. Messages like "You're a strong Black woman" come from the heart but leave us in the emotional bind of believing we always have to be strong or else we've failed. Being strong all the time is a burden and doesn't leave us much room to be human. When we can't live up to everybody's idea or expectation of a strong Black woman, we feel like a failure, and feeling like a failure only leads to big-time depression. It would be nice to have some room for emotional flexibility, but often we don't have a clue as to what emotional flexibility looks like for ourselves.

Hi, everybody, I'm Angie. Sometimes I just get so fed up with everything, including myself. It's like folks expect me to be like every other Black woman they know. I dropped out of college 'cause I couldn't afford to continue after I got pregnant with Kai, my little girl. My parents keep telling me I've just thrown my life away, 'cause I didn't do things the way they wanted me to do them. Hey, I'm twenty-two years old, with a three-year-old-child and I'm on state aid, but as soon as Kai starts school, I intend to start taking classes again. It will be hard, but I know I can do it.

It's really tough to explore and understand our individual identities when we continually receive messages from our parents, relatives, friends, and mainstream society about who we're suppose to be as Black women. The messages are often subtle but very potent in their effects on us. Messages like "being a Black women must mean that you're physically and emotionally strong"; "being on welfare means that you're shiftless and lazy"; "having children out of wedlock must mean you're a tramp"; or "being abused in some way means you asked for it, or don't deserve anything better." These types of messages cut deep into our psychological souls. We hear and mentally interpret these messages as expectations, and sometimes we even turn these expectations into self-fulfilling prophecies. My friend Lestine, a thirty-eight-year-old, single mother of three preteen kids, was depressed for months after being laid off from her job as a carpenter's assistant. Now Lestine makes good money when she's working, but the work is seasonal, and let's face it, when you've got three kids to clothe, feed, and keep warm, there's no such thing as good money, and prices these days don't allow for rainy-day savings. Anyway, Lestine revealed to me that while being laid off for several months at a time was difficult, it wasn't nearly as hard as having to secretly (keeping it from her parents and some friends) apply for welfare to feed and shelter herself and the kids during the lean times. Lestine explained that she felt bad about having to be on welfare, because the only thing she ever heard from her family when she was growing up was "Girl, you ain't go'n to amount to diddly-squat."

You know I feel so proud of myself when I'm working. I can thumb my nose at everybody, 'cause I'm showing them that they're wrong about me. But when I'm between jobs and on welfare it's like their predictions about me are true. They expected me to fail, and if they knew about my being on welfare part of the time, they would shake their heads and say, "See, I told you so," and that would hurt even more.

I told Lestine, quoting a prominent motivational speaker:

"Someone's opinion of you does *not* have to be your reality."

Lestine felt good when she could show her family that she wasn't a failure. But the sad part is, on an emotional level, she believed their earlier message that she was a failure.

Lestine's family's predictions and expectations for her were not her reality. She did prove them wrong, which I personally believe to be the best revenge. However, when things got tough, and things get tough for everybody from time to time, Lestine gave up what she knew to be true about herself, which was the proven fact that she was competent and capable of taking care of herself and her kids. Choosing to apply and get welfare during the down time didn't prove that she was a failure, it proved that she was resourceful.

When I asked Lestine how sometimes she managed to get past her family's negative predictions for her, she responded, "Well, I never really think about them at other times. But I knew I had to feed my kids, so I just told myself, I can do this. I just believed in me."

I strongly encouraged Lestine to hold onto that belief, even saying it out loud to herself, during the up times and down times.

I hear what you're say'n, sis, but it's not my family's messages that get me down as much as it is everybody else's messages.

This is Flo, a forty-seven-year-old, divorced parent of five children. Right now only two teenagers are at home. One daughter is away at college, and one son and one daughter are married. Flo's been working at the post office for twenty-three years. Did I get it right, Flo?

It's all there. Anyway, as I was say'n, it's like the only real Black women that folks see are on T.V. And according to Hollywood I'm supposed to dress like Tina Turner, dance like Janet Jackson, sing like Whitney Houston, and have a career like Claire what's-her-name on the Cosby show. And if I don't match any of those stereotypes, then I'm supposed to be on welfare, 'cause that's how we colored women supposed to be, right? Sometimes I swear the only thing that keeps me from cussing out those folks on my job is they don't have a clue about who I am, and I only have to be around them for eight hours at a stretch.

Flo's right! There are so many expectations about Black women that the "me" in each one of us can get lost in the daily shuffle.

The toughest challenge we will ever face as Black women will be holding onto the "me" in our individuality. The negative messages and expectations that we receive from our families, friends, and mainstream society don't go away when we're feeling good about ourselves. It's just that we don't give those negative messages a lot of our attention. But when things get tough, it's as if we turn up the volume on every negative message that we've ever heard about ourselves.

I have a hard time giving myself messages because I'm always thinking about what everyone else will say

or think, especially my folks. Every once in a while I can
tell myself something good, but it just doesn't last long.
*   Even when my friends say good things about me, it's*
like I don't really believe them. Oh yeah, I'm Janet; I go
to beauty school; I've been dating my boyfriend, Mark,
a year; and I don't have any children.

I believe that we're all born with enough personal self-
esteem messages to last us a lifetime. But when these
messages don't get nurtured when we are children, they
become almost nonexistent when we are adults. Just as
our infant and childhood bodies need care, nurturing, and
stimulation in order to help us grow into healthy adults,
our self-esteem needs the same type of care in order to
remain a healthy part of our lives.

I was born a writer; of course, my parents weren't
aware of this fact at the time of my birth. It was and still is
at times hard for me to believe in my talents as a writer
because the messages I often received were mixed and
unclear. Messages like "You can be anything you want to
be" fed my sense that I was lovable and worthwhile. Messages like "That's nice, but you better do something that's
going to feed you" fed my self-doubt. My parents, teachers, and friends didn't intend any harm—they were concerned about my future, so they encouraged and
supported what they thought was the practical part of my
growth. As I grew older, it became increasingly clear that
no matter how good I felt about myself in other parts of my
life, there was something missing, an empty space that
needed to be filled. My childhood self-doubt messages
were strong, and they started interrupting and overpow-
ering the few self-esteem messages I had managed to
keep. When I decided to take the risk and started writing,
I noticed that my empty space started to fill up. But at the
same time, my self-doubt increased. The first time a pub-
lisher asked to publish one of my stories my self-doubt
was so strong I threw up for two days. Yet I couldn't stop
writing, because I needed that empty space to be filled. It

became clear that in order to continue writing I would have to first rewrite my personal self-esteem messages. Let's face it, throwing up just ain't that much fun. While I was working on re-creating my self-esteem messages, I noticed that my self-doubt kept harassing me. Messages like "Who do you think you are?" or "How can I be a writer, I can't spell?" jumped out at me at every turn. Let me tell you, girlfriend, my self-doubt was doing some serious creep'n. This will probably happen to you too, so let me give you an idea of how self-doubt works.

In the morning, when I get in my car, the first thing I do is turn on my favorite FM station to keep me company on my twenty-mile commute to my office. Now, when I leave the house, the station is clear as a bell, and then after about five miles, I start to notice some static. At first the static is fairly low, and I can still hear my tunes, but the closer I get to work the louder the static becomes. By the time I'm about three miles from work, the static is so loud that it drowns out the music. At that point, I have four choices: continue listening to the static; change the station; pop in a tape; or turn the radio off. Since I don't function well without my tunes, I choose to pop in a tape.

Now, in a roundabout way, rewriting my self-esteem messages worked in the same way. When I first started the process, my self-doubt messages kept creating static, trying to overpower my new messages, "I can do this" and "I'm a worthwhile person." I noticed that the static crept in only when I was not consistent about giving myself the new messages. When I gave myself the new messages every day, it was like popping in a tape—the static didn't have a chance.

Do I still get the static from the old messages? Yes, but not as often, and my new messages are growing stronger every day. My proof is I haven't thrown up in a long time!

Now listen up, 'cause I'm going to say it again, just like I said it before, and I'm going to keep on saying it, 'cause it's the most important thing I can say. The only way to cut through everybody's messages is by giving ourselves more powerful messages. When the static of self-doubt creeps in, the most important messages we can give ourselves are **"I'm lovable"** and **"I'm worthwhile."** These two simple messages won't make us media stars, nor will they make others accept us. However, they will affirm our right to be ourselves as Black women, and they will cut through the unhealthy messages that feel burdensome.

Here's a little trick that helped me to start cutting through the static of my old messages. **On a small index card, I wrote, "I'm lovable" and "I'm worthwhile"; then I taped it to my bathroom mirror.** That card is the first thing I see in the morning and the last thing I see before I go to bed at night. I can't help how others choose to see me, but I can do something about how I see myself. **Saying those two sentences is the reward I give myself for being just who I am.** As I said before, I can't promise you'll become a Black princess or Janet Jackson, but I can promise you'll notice a difference in yourself. After all, this is Black magic we're talk'n about, in the truest sense of the word.

PART TWO

▼▲▼▲▼▲▼▲▼

HOMETRAINING

4

▼▲▼▲▼

Before Our Time

Mama, as my grandmother is respectfully called, doesn't put a lot of stock in the concept of self-esteem. In fact, what we call "self-esteem" Mama calls "Bible teaching," proper hometraining and common sense rolled into a fancy word. In truth, if something isn't Bible-certified, Sis Annie Dunn (my grandmother) don't want to hear about it. Mama's method of child-rearing was basic and for the most part fairly rigid: a well-worn Bible in the bedroom, a peachtree switch in every corner, plenty of food on the table, and clean clothes in every closet. These essentials provided the structure she needed for getting her babies (as her grandchildren are affectionately called) through life.

As is the custom in many Southern Black families, Mama shared our family home for long periods of time. Daddy's job required extensive travel, and raising nine children often necessitated more than the good Lord's help. Momi, my mother (Mama's second-oldest daughter), and Daddy never questioned Mama's child-rearing practices out of respect for her wisdom, but more so out of respect for the loyalty of tradition and a strong sense of what was familiar.

Both my mother and my father were raised by deeply religious Southern parents. From their parents my parents learned the basics of life: the Bible got you into heaven, strong discipline taught you respect, and common sense kept you alive. Self-esteem wasn't the issue for my parents or their parents. Survival was their primary goal.

As a child, I was never directly told that I was loved, but then again it never occurred to me to ask the question. In our house, love was an assumed notion as opposed to a spoken reality. I knew that Jesus loved me because the Bible told me so, and as a child I was taught that even Jesus' love was conditional, meaning that I had to be good so that I could get into heaven to receive his reward of love.

The concept of loving one's self was a foreign concept to my parents, because it was a foreign concept to their parents. I once heard a great teacher say, you can teach others only to the extent of your own knowledge; in this regard, my parents gave to me what had been given to them. The unfortunate news is that the traditional ethnic structure that helped my parents to survive their lives and sustained me through childhood falls short of what I need in today's world as a mature adult.

The majority of us had parents who were good at fulfilling our physical needs. They gave us what had been given to them, the courage to survive.

Our parents' teachings have served us well. We've learned and practiced the basic concepts of survival. However, we are beginning to recognize that our lives have moved a measure or two beyond the basic concepts.

I guess I'm lucky. I've got more than my parents ever had. I'm a professional, own my home, new car— all "the perks," as they say. But it's like I'm never satisfied with myself. When I stop to think about myself, I can't help but believe that something is missing.

We just heard from JoLinda, or "Jo" as she likes to be called. Jo is a contracts attorney for a major firm. Jo is forty-two, has two little girls ages nine and eleven, and she's engaged to be married.

Like Jo, as Black women today we've encountered a

phenomenon that was totally foreign to our mothers—the luxury of time for ourselves. True! We don't always recognize that we have personal time, nor do we use it, but it's there if we want to take advantage of it. It's not that our mothers didn't want to take personal time; there just wasn't room to fit it into their lives. My mother's idea of a convenience food was self-rising flour, and I go into a state of panic if the microwave goes on the blink. Let's face it, ladies, advanced modern technology has given us permission to take all the time we need in order to know ourselves a little bit better.

> *I hear what you're say'n, but even with modern conveniences I've still got two kids at home, a job, and a house to run. Yeah, I've got the things my mother didn't have, but I still don't have time for myself. And even if I did, I wouldn't know what to do with it.*
>
> —*Flo*

Again, we've learned the basics—how to do for others. The new lesson is how to do for ourselves. Because our mothers didn't have the advantages we have today, they learned to derive pride and pleasure from doing for others. "My duty is to do for ya'll, I'll get my rewards (in heaven) later" was Mama's standard reply whenever she was encouraged to sit down and take a load off.

We've learned to substitute our mothers' reality—the lack of personal time—with personal guilt if we choose to take time for ourselves. As a child, I learned early on never to utter the words "I'm bored" in earshot of any adult, because the guaranteed response was "Bored! What business you got being bored, with all this work 'round here wait'n to be done?" and a long verbal list of what needed to be done followed. The message was clear: Fill every minute of every waking hour.

Our lessons in basic survival skills also held the hidden message that doing for others should be our ultimate reward, and because we had vigilant teachers, we again learned our lessons well. We do for our families, our employers, our churches—for everyone but ourselves.

Even when I try to do something for myself, I always end up doing for everybody else, 'cause I feel bad if I don't. Like the other day I had a few extra dollars, so I bought this pair of shoes I've been want'n. On the way home I kept think'n about this jacket LaShawn's been want'n, and how I kept tell'n her I didn't have the money. And here I was with these shoes. You know I got off that bus at Southcenter and bought that girl that jacket which I really couldn't afford, just so I could keep my shoes in peace.

—Vy

Vy is thirty-eight years old, divorced, has fourteen-year-old twin sons and a sixteen-year-old daughter. She's an assembly-line supervisor at a local factory. And she's very proud of the fact that she's had fifteen months of being free from alcohol and drugs.

Like Vy, many of us mentally stumble over our daily responsibilities even when we try to do something for ourselves. We're experts at telling ourselves to do for the kids, husbands, lovers, employers, and friends, but it's time to start asking ourselves, "What do I need?" Too often we find ourselves feeling frustrated, angry, and let down because we neglect to make ourselves a major priority in the self-care department.

Yeah, but, sis, that's how I got in trouble in the first place. I was think'n about myself first when I was using the drugs and alcohol.

—Vy

We don't have to choose abuse as a form of self-care. I do believe that some sisters turn to alcohol and drug abuse out of frustration, hurt, and anger, in the belief that they are taking care of themselves. However, if we take care of ourselves before those feelings overwhelm us, then it's easier to avoid the abusive measures. Vy's decision to buy and keep her shoes was a decision to take care of herself in a healthy way.

No one is ever going to give us permission to take care of ourselves, so that means we have to be responsible for our own self-care. In a way it's selfish not to take care of ourselves, because in order to be at our best for those who depend on us, it means we have to be at our best—you guessed it—for ourselves.

Hi, everybody, I'm LaTisha, I have two kids— Monte, four, and Shawna, two. I live with my mother and I just started community college and I'm nineteen years old. My comment is everything costs so much, I would love to do self-care by being able to go out with my friends once in a while. Mama says she doesn't mind watching the kids. But my friends want to go to these expensive dance clubs. By the time I get something to wear there's no money left to party.

Things *are* expensive, but that doesn't mean we have to deprive ourselves of pleasures. One idea that comes to mind for LaTisha might be to suggest to her friends that each of them take turns selecting where they're going and how much they're willing to spend.

Taking care of ourselves doesn't always equal spending money, but it does mean spending time on the most important person we will ever have the pleasure to know.

It's pretty much like we discussed in the beginning— somewhere between selfish and selfless is self-care, which equals higher self-esteem. We've never learned how to make ourselves a priority, because that lesson wasn't available to our teachers (our mothers). Our basic teaching tells us that thinking and doing for ourselves is "selfish." Our current reality tells us that something is missing from our lives, even when we do for others, leaving us to feel "selfless." Self-care will teach us how to take care of what's important: *ourselves.*

Our mothers have given us the basics; advanced technology has provided the time; now it's up to us to continue our education. The lessons we'll learn are new and will require practice, but we've already proven to ourselves that we're excellent students.

5

▼▲▼▲▼

Family Legacies

I love my family, but Lord they sure do make me tired. Daddy's heart ain't good. Mama's git'n on in years and just can't take the load like she used to. My oldest sister's got four mouths to feed by herself. Junior's out there act'n the fool, strung out on that mess, and Baby Sis, well she's doing better but she's got a big-time alcohol problem. I haven't even told them my plans to leave Jimmy, 'cause it would just lead to more confusion than it's worth. I know they would be there for me if they could, but mostly everybody's sit'n around wait'n on the other shoe to drop. I'm so tired of wait'n on that shoe to fall, 'til sometimes I just want to knock it off.

That was our friend Tess. She asked to join our group because she just moved here from Maryland six months ago and has been feeling the need for friendship and support. Tess is forty-three and recently separated from her husband after twenty years of marriage. She has a fifteen-year-old daughter and a ten-year-old son. Tess works as a retail clerk in a department store.

Tess, I hope, will find in the group what I have found: unconditional support. My "family of choice" fulfills the needs that my biological family can't fulfill. The common thread that holds my sister circle together is the same thread that will bring us closer together.

Say some more about this unconditional support. Does it mean that your family—parents, brothers, and sisters—don't love you, and the women in the group love you more? I'm a little confused, 'cause I know my family loves me and I love them.

—Flo

Receiving unconditional support means that you're accepted just as you are right now, without having to emotionally sacrifice or physically change who you are as an adult woman. Our families do love us, but often their love is centered around their picture of us—big or little sister, dependable sister, and the like—as opposed to our own pictures of ourselves as adult women.

Excuse me, my name is Cassie and I know just what you're talking about. My family tells me all the time that they're proud of me as an artist, and that I can count on them for emotional support. But when that support really counts they let me down. Last week is a good example. My sister calls and invites me to Mom's birthday party. And then she says, "I'll even make an appointment for you at the hairdressers, 'cause we want everybody to look nice for the family pictures. And dress nice 'cause all of Mom's church friends are going to be here. I'm twenty-four years old, and I've been on my own teaching at the preschool for four years. The way she talked to me, you would think I was one of those kids at my preschool. Now how does she think those statements made me feel? I wear my hair in dreads and dress the way I do because it's an expression of who I am. The name of their game is—Be the same as us, or you're not one of us. That's some kind of support.

Cassie is feeling firsthand the conditional acceptance of her biological family. The message is clear: We can accept you only if you meet our expectations based on sameness. Ethnically different yet culturally the same is our family legacy as Black women. We receive this subtle yet potent message—You're just as good as they (meaning white folks), but you're not better than the rest of us, and don't you forget it—in our daily lives as children, and we carry bits and pieces of the legacy into our adult world.

To this very day, I hate the feel of Vaseline on my skin. Mama used to grease us from head to foot, in her never-ending battle to keep us from looking ashy. It was like it's okay to be black, but don't be ashy black, be shiny black, 'cause white folks don't understand ashy black. I always wanted to ask, What's the difference, Mama? 'cause I would see white folks treat ashy black folks the same way they treated shiny black folks.

—Vy

Even when we understand the inconsistent messages, they take on a life of their own in our adult world. Messages such as don't talk or laugh too loud. Don't wear bright colors, don't talk back, don't roll your eyes, don't slur your words, and above all, don't act "colored," but don't forget where you come from. In their own way, our parents were preparing us to live in two separate and unequal worlds. In one world, we were expected to act as if we were as good as or better than the "other" folks. It was our job to speak proper, dress correctly, and behave according to standards that required us to reject our ethnicity.

My father used to always tell us kids to act civilized whenever we got ready to leave the house. We all knew he meant for us to be on our best behavior. When I think about it now, he was really telling us to act like white folks. Shoot! If we had acted like some of those little white kids we saw in the stores, we would have gotten a killing when we got home.

—Jo

At home the messages were more relaxed but still based on a degree of sameness that declared your family kinship.

> *I stopped eating meat when I was fifteen, and I thought my family was going to have a fit. My brothers accused me of trying to be white. And my mother made this big thing of telling me she wasn't going to cook any special meals. I was expected to eat just what she fixed or eat nothing at all. I was made to feel like I committed some sin against the race, just 'cause I didn't want to eat meat. Can you believe that mess?*
>
> *—LaTisha*

Our famililies expect us to be loyal to them, and their vision of Blackness is their ultimate legacy. This legacy of Black-womanhood-sameness is a blessing and a curse. The blessing is that in our ethnicity and our womanhood we share a sense of connection and we have a history that can be traced to queens and rulers of empires. We can take pride in our heritage. The curse is that we're expected not to deviate from the mold of how we are supposed to be as Black women. It's expected that our loyalty to our race must and should override our loyalty to our individuality as women, as if we could automatically separate the two intertwining segments of our lives.

"Remember who you are [Black woman] and don't you ever forget it." These words were generally uttered as a warning by my mother, whenever she felt my opinions or sense of ethnic loyalty were out of line. My mother's words were meant as a reminder that my thinking wasn't meeting her expectations of what a proper Black woman should believe. I never had the nerve to answer (at least in earshot anyway), "But, Momi, how could I be anything else but a Black woman?"

Whenever I attempted to do or say something that didn't fit with my family's degree of sameness, I heard the ever-immortal words: "When you get grown you can do whatever you want in y*our* house, but as long as you live in *this* house you'll do as I say." As an adult I've come to recognize that my body is in a sense my house, and while the foundation has a very solid base (my biological family), the structure (physical appearance), rooms (personality), and furnishings (individuality) are very much of my own choosing. My family is very proud of my "home" (me), but as it is with most families, they will often make suggestions and offer opinions, comments, and advice for improvements. You know, things like "You should wear your hair this way," or "That dress is too short (or too long)," "You need to lose (or gain) weight," or "You weren't raised to talk or act that way." My family's suggestions for "home" improvements come from their heart—they love me. But my family doesn't always understand me, and to some degree that makes them very uncomfortable with me, because my house is laid out differently than theirs. When I first moved away from home, "doing my own thing," and went back for visits, I would work my butt off trying to get them to accept "the new, improved, individualized, adult version of me"—of course I had much more emotional energy in those days. Now when I look at my memories of those times I understand that I was really asking my family to change their "house" (their personalities) in order to make me more comfortable. I needed and expected my family to be different as a way of validating the changes I had made for myself. We used to get into some real tug-of-war disputes over who I am versus who they needed me to be. "What's wrong with you, you've changed?" "I know, it's for the better." "No, it isn't." "Yes, it is." And so on and so forth.

Over the years, I've grown more emotionally mature. This is in large part because I've discovered a number of ways in which I can be validated and be accepted for the woman I am today. And, my sisters group has been an important part of this. I no longer depend on my family alone for the degree of unconditional support that allows me to be an individual. This change took some time and a lot of major family discussions (and I might add that we're not always in agreement). But the upshot is that, when I'm with family members, I respect their choices, beliefs, and needs to live their lives in the manner that makes them feel most comfortable. And, for the most part, they respect me in kind. Do I have to give up a part of my home (myself) in order to be in my family's presence? Yes. While we're together, I have to close some of the doors to rooms (thoughts and ideas) that would make their lives and mine much too uncomfortable. But I close those doors willingly in their presence because I know that in other areas of my life I'll have the freedom to swing those doors wide open and even redecorate if I so choose. Does my family know that those closed rooms exist? Yes, they know. They even sometimes ask to take a peek: "Why don't you believe in spanking?" or "Do you still date interracially?" But for the most part they respect my arrangements, as long as they can identify and feel comfortable in some parts of the house. With me, as with many of us, the love and acceptance of family are important. Because of that need, and again, because I have other sources of support, I'm willing to give my family a degree of recognizable family sameness that supports their need and mine for love, unity, and loyalty.

Another beautiful and very powerful example of how family loyalties and legacies come into question is illustrated in this scene from the late Lorraine Hansberry's play *A Raisin in the Sun*. Beneatha, the saucy, exotic, worldly daughter, explains to her matronly, God-fearing mother how she (Beneatha) doesn't accept, or believe in, the idea of God. Her mother gives Beneatha several serious warnings: "Beneatha, it don't sound nice to say such things," and, "Beneatha, you weren't raised that way," which Miz Beneatha chooses not to take seriously. Then Mama feels she has no choice but to slap Miz Beneatha straight and have her humbly repeat the words, "In my mother's house there is still God." Mama finishes her reprimand with "There are some ideas we ain't going to have in this house."

Many of us, like Beneatha, have had our individuality literally and figuratively slapped out of us, because it just wasn't acceptable to be different in thought, word, or deed.

Whenever I try to act different or be more individual, everybody tells me I'm acting stuck on myself. It's like my family and friends expect me to be the same all the time. But I'm not the same person all the time, I need to break out of the shell every once in awhile just so I know I'm alive.

—Della

I know just what you're say'n, Della. I have the same problem. My family thinks that just because I'm an attorney I'm supposed to know all the answers to life's problems. Sometimes I think that my family only wants to see me as a professional, but it's like hey wake-up folks, I'm human too, with needs, wants, and desires just like everybody else.

—Jo

Being an individual means that we all operate on different levels of our personalities in different situations. For example, in the office I'm more businesslike—after all, that's what I'm there for, "to take care of business"; with some friends I tend to be more informal but not totally crazy; around my parents and other family members I tend to be endearingly respectful—sometimes my "craziness" slips out, but what can I say, we're family.

We all need at least one safe place to talk, laugh, cry, and feel connected without the burden of having to present ourselves in a certain manner. Having a group large or small of sisters, a "family of choice," who can accept us just as we are, can be one of the ways we choose to give ourselves self-care.

> *Hi, everybody, I'm Maxine, I'm thirty years old, married and have four children at home. I've been teaching at the high school for eleven years, and I've been attending Mt. Baptist Church for fifteen years, and while I have social associations in both of those places, there's only about two or three of those women, at the most, that I could say I was really close enough to, to really share myself in a personal way. And you say it takes time, how much time? Because with lesson plans and running a family and home my time is always in short supply.*

If you have two or three trusted friends, that's all it takes. Most of us already have a couple of people that we're close to and share things with at present. But be open to meeting and inviting other women from work, school, or church to join the group. Truly trusting each other does take time, and the major focus is on accepting each other's differences while being able to honor your own differences in the security of having ethnic sameness. Sometimes it helps to build trust when you have a couple of things in common. In our group, all of us love to read and the majority of us are writers. When we first got together, we mostly discussed the different books we had read or the writing project we were working on at the time. Right away, we noticed that we enjoyed reading different authors, and we all practiced different styles of writing. Some of us write poetry, some of us write children's works, some of us write novels. As we got to know and trust each other over a period of time, we discovered that we felt comfortable revealing other similarities and differences with each other. We would also bring and introduce other sisters to the group. Some of the other sisters aren't writers, but they love to read, which again gives us some common ground on which to start building our trust as a group. As artists in their own right, these nonwriting sisters have given and received the gift of unconditional support within our circle.

As far as time is concerned, yes, having a support group requires time, but you get to decide how much or how little time you choose to spend. There's no need for an agenda, dues, or hassle and fluff; the only requirement is time and the willingness to come together on a regular basis. Our strongest ties are our love and support of each other. As adult women we're able to create new and exciting legacies for ourselves, which we can pass along to our young sisters.

The pain, pressure, joy, and love of family legacies are a part of our history as Black women. However, as adults we can make choices about how our family legacies will and will not affect our individual lives.

Take some time to reflect on what types of family legacies were handed down to you as a Black woman. How do these legacies serve you now as an adult? What part of your history do you want to pass on to your daughters, nieces, younger sisters? The idea and act of change will be a challenge because change may mean that you have to give up some form of family sameness and thus lose a degree of emotional support. But a challenge can be exciting over time, and as an individual you have all the time you need to change. Remember, as a Black woman you possess the courage to accept the challenge of being yourself.

6

▾▴▾▴▾

Starting from Scratch

If someone had asked my parents when we were young, which of their nine children would be successful, I doubt seriously if my name would have escaped their lips. I was a sickly, skinny, awkward, sassy child with a lot of mouth and no backup. I loved books and hated school, and "why is that" started all of my sentences.

Bless her heart, Momi tried her hardest to instill all of the basic ladylike qualities in her six girls. You know, stuff like a clean house is a happy house, the joy of cooking, and never ever talking with your mouth full. I guess she just offered me up as her ultimate sacrifice. She used to say, "If I can deal with you, the rest are a piece of cake." This remark usually came after she discovered my sisters' willingness to do my work—fifty cents went a long way in those days—while I hid out in the bathroom with a book. The quickest way to get Daddy to volunteer to take us all out for Sunday dinner was to casually announce after church that it was my turn to cook (that saying about all Black women being good cooks really is a myth when it comes to me). So it's understandable why my parents wouldn't pick me as the family frontrunner.

Actually, when I look back at my childhood years, I see that I was a ripe candidate for low self-esteem as an adult. There were low periods in those years, like all the times I spent on the seventh floor of Skin and Cancer Hospital with severe outbreaks of eczema, or when I failed the third grade because of lengthy absences for illness and the kids poked fun of me. Even today, some thirty-five years later, the pain of those memories makes me shudder. But just as I have memories of those low times, I also have memories of the high times, like the time I threw myself a surprise tenth birthday party and invited all of my friends. At the appointed hour, everyone showed up, dressed to the teeth, gifts in hand, only to surprise my very unsuspecting parents. Later that evening, after everyone left with memories of a good time on their lips, my mother wanted to know what in the world made me throw myself a surprise party. And of course I responded in my typical sassy fashion that I thought being two numbers (one and zero) instead of one number seemed like a special thing, and I wanted everybody to be happy with me. I can still see Momi shaking her head as she replied, "Lord, child, what am I going to do with you?"

Memories are nothing more than very powerful thoughts that are attached to experiences, situations, or events that occur in our lives. The view that we have of ourselves today as adults is often based in large part on our childhood memories of ourselves. When things in our lives are going fine, we rarely give much, or any, thought to our childhood experiences. However, when we have adult experiences that cause us personal pain, it's not uncommon for us to examine past childhood memories in hopes of finding an answer to relieve our present pain. We do what I call the "if only" dance, as in "if only I had better parents" or "if only I had learned to cook" (this used to be one of my personal favorites).

While it's true that some childhood experiences, such as physical or sexual abuse, cannot and should not be overlooked in the shaping of our adult development, most memories don't have to control our adult self-esteem. As adults we have something we didn't have as children: the power of choice. Nikki Giovanni, a gifted Black poet and writer, clearly states, **"Power only means the ability to have control over your life. Power implies choice."**

As adults our power lies in our ability to have a healthy sense of self. Self-esteem is power. As children we don't have power, and therefore our ability to make choices is limited, if it exists at all. We can't change our childhood memories or experiences—what's done is done; however, we can decide whether we allow our adult selves to be held hostage to the past. Here's a case in point.

For much of my adult life, I held myself hostage because of my eczema. Every time I allowed stress to creep in, my eczema broke out—talk about a vicious cycle. Whenever my skin broke out, I would have the painful childhood memories of being in the hospital, probing doctors, and taunting kids, and these memories would leave me feeling totally helpless and powerless as an adult. I forgot that as an adult I had choices about how I viewed myself as a whole person, and I didn't have to rely on only one view of myself. I could choose to view myself as a loving mother, as a woman who loves to shop till she drops, as a woman who enjoys sharing time with close friends, as a professional. I was all of these women even when my skin wasn't perfect. Over time, through much trial and error, as I started learning more about myself as a competent adult, I learned that I could let go of my former belief that I wasn't acceptable as a whole person because of my skin condition. My fear about not being perfect, which for me was based on the condition of my skin, cost me a lot of valuable time and emotional energy. I learned that my fears were nothing more than F.E.A.R.: Fantasies Expecting A Reality. No one ever actually told me that I wouldn't or couldn't have a loving relationship, a career, a child, or loving and nurturing friends if I had eczema. Those were *my* ideas, and those ideas weren't real because I had all of those things, plus a lot more. The eczema comes and goes, but I still have my relationship (that comes and goes too, but that's another story), my child, my career, and my friends. The proof of my reality blew my fears out of the window.

When I was a child, no one told me that I had a choice about how I viewed my illness. I received the message, mostly unspoken, that my skin condition made me different. When my skin was clear, I interpreted *different* as being special. At times like this, I felt so good I could throw myself a surprise party. Sometimes, generally when my skin broke out, I interpreted *different* as being hopeless and helpless. Because so much attention was directed toward making me well, I had learned to believe that my skin represented me: everything about me was tied up in my skin. I carried this childhood belief into adulthood and fashioned my life accordingly. Learning more about myself and learning how to manage my stress overload provided me with new information that allowed me to rethink and thus challenge my original childhood self-image.

> *I've always loved bright colors, reds, yellows—all the colors I think are pretty. But I don't wear them because when I was young I was always told, "You can't wear bright colors 'cause you're too dark." Now even when I wear red lipstick and somebody gives me a compliment, I feel so self-conscious that I go and wipe it off.*
> —Callie

> *Everybody in my family called me Olive Oyl 'cause I was tall and skinny. Then when I was ten I had to get glasses 'cause of this problem with my right eye. One of my friends was over to my house one day, and she heard my brother call me four-eyes. She started calling me that at school, and it made everybody laugh at me. To this day, whenever I hear a person call somebody four-eyes or Olive Oyl, I get this sick feeling in the pit of my stomach, 'cause I think they're talking about me.*
> —Janet

Both of these sisters are being held hostage by childhood recollections that they're using to construct adult images of themselves. Often we don't even notice that we're holding ourselves hostage until a situation or event triggers the stored memory we have of ourselves. When that memory is triggered, it releases a flood of feelings associated with the memory. For example, when I remember—some thirty years later—the look of surprise on my parents' faces when they saw all those kids at the door for my surprise party, I smile. And when I'm stressed out and my eczema acts up, I feel vulnerable and scared because I remember doctors and long hospital stays. At these times, I have to remind myself quickly that I'm not seven years old and I have choices about how to handle this situation.

We can break away from childhood memories that threaten our adult self-esteem, but first—and this is the hard part—we have to become more aware of situations and events that trigger old memories that leave us feeling helpless. Once we discover which situations or events cause us to feel helpless, we can, by adding new information that will help us feel more powerful, challenge whatever memory we're having. This may sound confusing, so let me explain how the whole process works.

Memories are nothing more than past thoughts, and our thoughts are pictures we have of ourselves. Unless we choose to share what we're thinking, our thoughts are very private—no one has the ability to read our minds. When our thoughts are strong enough, they can have a powerful effect on our feelings. For example, when I'm stressed out and my eczema acts up, I have memories (thoughts) of being sick as a child. I actually have a mental picture of being small, alone, and crying in a huge white iron hospital bed. This thought leaves me feeling helpless. The stressful *situation* is my eczema, the *thought* is being alone, and the *feeling* is helplessness. My current situation triggered a thought, which in turn had a direct impact on my present feelings. By learning how to do two things—(1) becoming more aware of and managing stressful situations, and (2) challenging my thoughts—I've learned how to feel more competent.

Managing my stress consists of learning how to set reasonable daily priorities, setting aside daily pleasurable time, and eating right. By taking positive action—"doing something" for myself—I was able to lower my stress level.

Learning how to challenge my thoughts took more effort, but the payoff is great and it works. First, I have to pay attention to the thought "I'll never be well," which triggers my feeling "helpless." Taking action, calling the doctor or putting on my skin creme, allows me to balance my negative thought with a positive one, "I can take care of myself," which leaves me feeling competent.

Try this exercise and see if it's helpful. I'm going to warn you up-front that it's going to take practice, so please be patient with yourself.

Picture yourself in a stressful situation—for example, getting a bank notice that your check bounced. Now observe your thought—"Oh my God! I can't do anything right" or "I'm so stupid. I can't even count." Now notice how you are feeling—panicked or discouraged. The thoughts are quick, so pay attention, and remember they're generally triggered by memories. I told you this was hard work. Now picture the same stressful situation, check bouncing, and this is the tricky part, balance the old thought with the image of yourself taking some type of action—calling the bank to get more information. Now notice your feeling—nervous but not panicky.

Now let's try it again just to see if you really get the idea of how challenging thoughts works.

Picture yourself after a heated argument with your husband or lover and that person slams out of the house. Notice your thought—"He's left me and he's never coming back. Oh my God, why did I say those things? I'm a fool. He's gone, and it's all my fault." Now notice your feelings—scared, ashamed, panicked, sad. Now image yourself taking some action—taking a shower, making a phone call, going for a walk. Now notice your feelings again—still sad but not panicked, ashamed but not scared. This would also be a good time to remember the acronym F.E.A.R.—Fantasies Expecting A Reality. Unless you have proof that your husband or lover isn't going to return, then your fear is a fantasy, and holding onto and believing the fantasy increases the feelings—in this case, panicked, scared, ashamed, and sad—that you associate with it. And, if he *doesn't* come back . . . you have a golden opportunity to find out that you amount to a lot more than one relationship.

Here's something else to think about, girlfriend, you are *not* your thoughts, and you are *not* your feelings. Thoughts and feelings are only a part of you as a total individual. You can always have options as to how you choose to think and feel about any given situation.

The idea of this exercise was to help you pay more attention to situations, thoughts, and feelings. By doing this exercise, you're giving yourself an option and letting in new information that will gradually allow you to move away from the old images of yourself. This next part is important and worth remembering. You won't forget the old image of yourself. Human nature and human brains just aren't that advanced, and creating a new image isn't akin to magic. What you're doing is giving yourself space to create a different, more powerful image of yourself. This process isn't going to happen overnight. Like I said before, it's going to take time and patience, but hey, what else have you got that's more important than yourself?

For those sisters who are resisting the urge to try this exercise (yes, I know you're out there reading this and expressing doubt), give yourself the benefit of at least trying this exercise for three weeks before tossing in the towel. Remember, believing that we're competent and powerful starts with *thinking* we're competent and powerful. And the time to start thinking that we're competent and powerful is *right now!*

7

▼▲▼▲▼

What Madness Brought Me Here?

I was halfway watching Oprah the other day, and she had these women on talking about how they had problems functioning in their adult lives because they came from dysfunctional families. Now, one woman had a problem with men, another woman couldn't hold a job, and another woman had problems with alcohol. Now, like I said, I was only halfway listening, but their upbringing didn't sound all that different than mine— one of them was even a sister. But they called their families dysfunctional, and I always thought my family was normal. What in the world is a dysfunctional family anyway?

—Jo

I'm go'n to ask ya'll to excuse me while I put on my therapist hat and shoes for this chapter. Explaining the ins and outs of a complex subject like family dysfunction takes a balanced head and steady feet. If I sound a tad bit dry, it's because I'm trying to get the message across in a clear, understandable way. Don't worry, though, it's still me talking.

The term *dysfunctional family* became widely used about ten or twelve years ago. While it was initially used in connection with drug and alcohol recovery programs, *dysfunctional family* is now commonly used to describe the families of those who've grown up in unhealthy or painful situations.

My family wasn't any better or any worse than any other family on the block. Hell, I grew up in the projects in Newark, New Jersey. When the eagle flew on Friday, you could bet your bottom dollar that somebody was going to get shot on Saturday. But M'dear took good care of us. She might of got loose on Saturday night, but she was there for us on Sunday morning. Now you all might call my family upbringing dysfunctional, but I ain't having none of it.

—Nettie

A large part of what determines a family's dysfunction is the impact it has on us as adults. While we are born with some coping behaviors, the majority of what we learn about coping with our personal world comes from our family role models.

I've got some serious confusion going on in my head about all this dysfunctional stuff. What are people actually talking about? I guess the reason I ask is because I'm fifty-two, and I'm a lesbian with five grown kids. I didn't come out till after my husband passed away a few years back, but the kids were already on their own by then anyway. But does my being who I am, even when I was with their father, mean that my kids were raised in a dysfunctional home? Oh, I almost forgot, I'm Bess, and I'm a nurse at City Hospital.

Talking about dysfunctional families without really knowing how to define *dysfunctional* is confusing, so let's break it down. Some coping styles are healthier than others. When I say "coping style," I'm speaking of ways in which family members handle the stresses of daily life in relation to other family members. Some obvious dysfunctions include a parent or other guardian drinking or using drugs to the point of neglecting his or her responsibilities; a parent acting sexually, physically, or verbally abusive toward other family members. Less obvious forms of abuse include emotional and physical neglect and verbal, emotional, and mental degradation. If any of these forms of abuse were present in your family on a consistent and continual basis, then it's fairly safe to say that your family was dysfunctional.

In answer to Bess's last question, No, your children weren't raised in a dysfunctional home because you're a lesbian, even if you had raised them with a female lover, instead of your husband—that is, unless some of the previously mentioned actions took place. The ways in which we choose to raise our children are not based on or dictated by our sexual orientation.

> *I've read and heard about the dysfunctional family syndrome, but somehow I got the impression that this was something that applied to white families. Growing up in my family it seemed like the first thing we all learned was that the family was sacred.*
>
> *—Nettie*

It would be nice to believe that our families were immune to dysfunctional behavior. But the bottom line is there's just too much concrete evidence to say otherwise. According to the latest national crime statistics, Black on Black crime is at an all-time high. More young Black sisters are turning to drugs and alcohol to relieve their personal pain. And the evidence of their pain is showing up. Hospitals are reporting a steady increase in the number of drug-addicted and HIV-positive infants born each year. While it's true that some social forces play a role in the lives of Black folks, much of what we experience in the way of personal victimization begins right in our homes. In the name of loving discipline, some of us suffered vicious and cruel beatings, or degrading personal insults and name calling. Sometimes our parents said this was done in order to shape us up as children, but seldom if ever does such abuse achieve the desired effect.

The physical and emotional scars received in childhood often erupt in our adult lives in the form of low self-esteem and occasionally total disregard for the lives of others. Someone once told me that if I didn't beat my son he would grow up to be homosexual. My response then remains the same today: I would be honored if my child chose to reflect and express his nonviolent upbringing with another person, be it man or woman. That choice shall remain his to make.

Making the decision not to hit or verbally put down my son was easy, but the follow-through was often difficult because I wasn't raised that way. First, it meant finding new ways to discipline, like time-out, and removing privileges for reasonable lengths of time. The most difficult part of my decision not to use physical or verbal force was convincing my family and getting their support to honor my decision. In defending my position, I would often hear "Who ever heard of raising a Black child without beating them" or "You must think your child is too good to hit." I truly believe that my son is worth the extra effort it took to get my point across. While I can't swear that my son has never been hit or verbally put down by others, I can say with a clear conscience that he's never experienced these acts from me. It's my hope that he will choose to reflect his upbringing when he interacts with others.

Our children are very prized and valuable gifts, and they deserve to be treated in that manner. It's funny, I often hear sisters saying things like "She's going to be sorry later on 'cause she's just spoiling that child" when referring to how another sister is lavishing attention on her child. Personally, I don't believe that children can spoil—fruits, vegetables, and meats spoil, and that's only if we don't take proper care of them. We can't spoil our children by showing them loving, nurturing care. Giving a child lots of emotional attention or even sometimes generous material gifts won't harm them. Raising our children with loving attention, dignity, and respect can only serve to enhance their lives, and hopefully they'll pass these lessons along to their children.

> *What about punishment? I don't beat my girls like I used to get beat. But every once in a while I'll take the belt to their legs. Personally, I think half of these kids out here get'n in trouble are doing it because they didn't have any discipline in the home.*
>
> *—Jo*

That's a good point, Jo, and you've mentioned two key words—*punishment* and *discipline.* Many of us, like so many of those kids on the streets in trouble, were punished. The word *punishment* implies harsh, cruel, sometimes sadistic treatment which is designed to humble, humiliate, and control the person being punished. Remember, it's like I said before, this type of punishment by its very nature is abusive and rarely if ever accomplishes its goal. On the other hand, *discipline* implies correcting behavior to teach or show an alternative form of doing something. Disciplining or correcting someone's behavior doesn't have to be or need to be physically, verbally, or emotionally painful. For older kids, taking away a privilege or restricting a favorite activity, and for younger children, time-out or removing a cherished toy for a limited time can achieve the desired effect, which is to correct the child's offending behavior. Always explain the reasons for your actions.

> *Shoot! I used to get my behind whipped with an ironing cord that left welts on me for days. And I turned out okay. I ain't no angel or nothing like that, but I ain't on the streets either. In fact I think I'm a better person because of those whippings.*
>
> *—Vy*

I once saw a button in a novelty shop that expressed this sentiment about capital punishment: "Why do we kill people who kill people to show that killing is wrong?" In a way, that same sentiment applies here. "Why do we hurt our children to show our children that their behavior is unacceptable?"

We're not better women because of the abusive treat-ment we received in the name of punishment, we're bet-ter women in spite of it. The only thing that the punishment taught us was how to alter our behavior. If we got a whipping because we got caught sneaking out of the house the first time, then we just made double-sure we didn't get caught sneaking out the next time. Check it out, less than 10 percent of the people in prison today are first-time offenders. If the punishments we received were more helpful than harmful, the issue of increasing our self-esteem would be a moot point. I don't believe that our parents or guardians intended to harm or hurt our emo-tional and psychological growth. Many of them were re-lying on methods of punishment that had been used to "shape them up." We have the knowledge about alterna-tive methods of disciplining our children, and we have the option of stopping this type of abuse.

"Sis, I need to say somethin' on this subject of how we treat our kids."

"Everybody, this is my friend Zoey. Do you want to introduce yourself, Zoey?"

"Eve' everybody, I'm Zoey, a long-time friend of sis's. Enough said. Now to state my point, earlier you were talk'n about groceries spoiling and not kids. Well, the way I see it, kids and groceries have at least one thing in com-mon—expiration dates. When groceries reach their expi-ration date and start spoiling we can throw them away. But when kids reach their childhood expiration date, they become adults and start having memories of their child-hood. We're livin' proof of that fact. We got to start think'n about what type of childhood memories we want our kids to have as adults."

Thanks, Zoey, you hit the mark on that one. We'll hear more about and from Zoey as we go along. She's a long-time, not-very-silent friend who keeps me on my toes.

Well, you certainly got my attention, but some of this is hard to swallow. Both of my parents were heavy drinkers, and there wasn't always enough money for extras, but they both worked and kept us kids clothed and fed. I put myself through college, and yeah, I get low sometimes, but who doesn't? But if what you say is true, shouldn't I be dysfunctional too?

—Maxie

While your family is the major influence in your life, it's by no means the only influence. As you grow older and start becoming more socially integrated, through school, church, and outside activities, you meet a number of people who influence your personal choices. You may be mentally, emotionally, and physically challenged in these situations. For example, watching a documentary on men in prison, hearing these men talk about how they were raised as children, motivated me to read articles and take classes on child care, which led to my decision on alternative forms of discipline. The more challenged you are the more you begin to see and notice differences that motivate you toward making choices and changes in your life.

Coming from a dysfunctional family doesn't mean you are dysfunctional. However, we know that often children who grow up in dysfunctional families carry that legacy into their adult lives. The dysfunctions often show up in the way these adults handle stress. Some of the dysfunctional ways of coping with stress might be:

- eating or drinking to excess
- using street drugs
- misusing prescription medications
- behaving abusively toward children, spouses, or others
- neglecting health or grooming

The pain doesn't stop there. Adults who were raised in dysfunctional families may have recurring, medically unexplained health problems. And they may suffer from ongoing depression.

> *From what you say, there aren't any normal families out there.*
>
> —Janet

Normal is a hard word to define. If you mean, "Are there any well-adjusted families?" the answer is yes. To some degree most families have some well-adjusted features, just as most families share some dysfunctional features.

Normal and *dysfunctional* are labels that describe a range of behaviors that affect individuals within the family unit. It's important to remember that it's your experience within the family unit that counts, not the label that describes your family.

Here's an exercise you might want to try to help you identify how you acquired some of the characteristics and behaviors you have as an adult.

Take a sheet of paper and a pencil, and draw a line down the center of the paper. At the top of the first half write, *My Characteristics and Behaviors.* At the top of the second half write, *I Learned This From.* On the first half write a list of all the characteristics and behaviors you can think of—the good, bad, and ugly. Spread them out so you'll have room to look them over. Then, on the second half, write the name of the family member from whom you believe you learned these characteristics. So the paper will look like this:

My Characteristics and Behaviors I Learned This From

Sense of humor	Daddy
Writing down my thoughts	Mommy
Buying anything on sale	Daddy

After you finish your list, put a star by the characteristics and behaviors you're proud of and want to keep or enhance. Put a check mark by the characteristics and behaviors you would like to change. Now turn the paper over. List the characteristics and behaviors that you want to change. Make a plan for how you would like to change that characteristic or behavior.

Characteristic and Behavior	*Plan to Make Change*
Overeating	Join Weight Watchers
Getting stressed out	Take ten-minute walks

Remember, girlfriend, we have the power to change, and this exercise is a step in that direction. Go for it!

8

▼▲▼▲▼

The Misinformation of Education

> I pass'd by the schoolhouse door even if I didn't go in.
>
> —Annie Dunn, my grandmother

"Don't be stupid, look it up" was a universal phrase in my house when I was a child. True, hearing this didn't do much for my self-esteem, but I sure did learn how to read in a hurry. In fair defense of my father, he generally resorted to such phrases only when his tension level was at its peak. In fact, Daddy encouraged us kids to ask questions. However, I seriously doubt if it occurred to him, a trained engineer who believed that all questions in the universe had logical answers, that nine children between the ages of eleven and two rarely if ever appreciated logical answers.

Actually, I used to believe that my father was a renegade schoolteacher, masquerading in engineer's clothing, especially when it came to reviewing our homework. Nothing brought tears to my eyes faster than seeing him whip out his trusty ballpoint pen at the mere sight of my freshly finished homework. I mean that man could diagram a sentence in his sleep. In fact, the only person he didn't mess with in terms of educational improvement was Cou'n Dunn, as he referred to my grandmother. The minute he would try to correct Mama, she would rear back in her chair, shoot him the evil eye, and stop him cold with "Look'a here, Joe Conyers, I pass'd by the schoolhouse door even if I didn't go in."

Yes, ma'am, Daddy was a real fanatic when it came to schooling of any kind. I was nearly eleven years old before I discovered that "they" (as in the proverbial "they say") weren't bona fide members of the family. Daddy quoted them so often I was sure we were related!

I'm telling you, statements like "This report card is okay, but next time I want to see all As" and "My job is to go to work and earn a living. Your job is to go to school and earn a decent education" were favorites of his. Then there was the real motivation enhancer: "I'm going to throw that idiot box [television] out of here if I don't start seeing some improvements in these grades." This last statement made me tremble in my shoes for a week.

Going to school wasn't a requirement in our house, it was a sacrament. And I'm fairly certain that if Daddy had his way "Thou shall covet formal education" would have been the first commandment, instead of falling in eleventh place, as it did in our house.

My parents, as most parents do, put great stock in the concept of formal education. They wanted us to do well in school because they believed that formal education was the key that opened the golden door to our mystical freedom. Our parents' premise about education was strong, but the reality of our education was weak.

Having a reasonable share of my father's genetic makeup puts me in the position of having a fair amount of respect for formal education. In fact, I'm pretty fascinated by the whole educational process. However, the stark realities of life as a Black female who survived the full regime of the public education system quickly brought home the fact that Mama wasn't the only Black woman who passed by the schoolhouse door.

The main thing I learned in school was that I didn't exist. Not as a student, a female, or a person of color. What I learned was that the American educational system, like

much of the society we live in, was never intended to educate or support our female gender or our ethnic diversity.
I also learned that schools were created, designed, and
implemented by white males in order to educate white
males. These indirect lessons began our first day of school
in "Teach Me 101," or, as it's more properly known, kin-
dergarten, with the lack of Black females in our studies. I
am sure this fact comes as no great surprise to those of us
who grew up cutting our reading teeth on the Dick and
Jane books, learning that Dick's main goal in life was
chasing Jane or seeing Spot run.

> *I loved school as a child, but as I got older it was
> harder and I just couldn't keep up. The teachers told
> my mother I was lazy and didn't apply myself. Every-
> body told me to study harder, but I really didn't know
> how to study to hold onto the information. It seemed to
> me like the harder I tried, the worse it got. So when I
> turned sixteen, I just gave up and dropped out.*
>
> —*Angie*

It's really not surprising that a high number of young
Black females fail and are pushed out, as opposed to drop
out, of an educational system that was never designed to
include us.

> *Whoa, sis, unless you're run'n for office, I'm missing
> the point here. This is about self-esteem, remember.*
>
> —*Flo*

While there might not seem to be a connection between education and personal self-esteem, they are pow-
erfully linked. The ways in which we were educated play
a major role in how we see ourselves as individuals. In
fact, outside of our families, school had the greatest impact on our personal lives. Ideally, our education should
have been the great equalizer in our very unequal world,
but the reality fell far short.

As Black women we never saw ourselves portrayed in history, literature, or science books. When Blacks were mentioned in these areas, they were males. The message was subtle and indirect but very clear: Black females just did not exist.

As young Black females, we learned we could not be astronauts, scientists, doctors, or attorneys. The basic underlying educational messages we received as Black women was "to be as much like the dominant culture as possible; otherwise you're invisible." Snow White and the Seven Dwarfs wasn't just an innocent fairy tale. It was an image we were given on which to start our early educational constructive learning. One of my first classroom images of blackness was introduced in the form of a story, *Little Black Sambo.* I can remember all of my little white classmates laughing as this little Black boy went running through the jungle with a skimpy cloth around his middle, trying to get away from a big scary tiger. My image of being a female was introduced in the form of Cinderella. This young innocent white girl is mistreated by her family, becomes friendly with rodents, goes to a ball where she's discovered by the prince, and ends up being carried off by him. Neither *Little Black Sambo* nor *Cinderella* fit Black women, but both of these images were used to start one of the most important processes in my life—my education to the world.

When we're given enough messages that tell us we're invisible and don't really count in the larger society, then we start believing them. As children, if we aren't given educational materials that help us to draw realistic images of ourselves, then it becomes difficult to view ourselves as competent and capable.

> *School wasn't that difficult for me. It wasn't like I was a straight A student, but I did okay. I finished high school and even finished a couple of years of college. Why wasn't I affected by all this stuff?*
>
> —*Cassie*

Many educators believe that early learning is based on the power of individuals to construct images or mental pictures of given information. It's generally believed that being able to construct the mental images makes the information real or more understandable. As we get older, we're introduced to more abstract forms of information such as math and the sciences, but to a large degree even those abstractions are grounded in our ability to construct mental images.

Many of us did well in school academically. The absence of ethnically diverse images didn't stop our learning process; it just made the transference of our educational process to our personal reality more difficult.

We start learning when we are born and can continue until we die. Educational experts know that the ability to connect new information to a person's current reality makes a powerful, lasting learning experience. That's why reading, one of the tools that we use to help us take in new information, is so important. Reading simulates lived experiences and helps us to build images. If we receive positive images about ourselves before we start school, we can substitute the negative or absent images with the positive images we've already learned.

When I was young, stories were a big thing in our house. Sometimes the stories came from books, but generally the stories centered around my parents' experiences as young children. Momi's stories always started with "When I was a little girl, about your age," and Daddy's tales began with "I remember when I was a boy." As a youngster, Daddy was quite the adventurer, running away from home, ditching school—you name it, he did it. Momi would tell us about growing up down South on the family farm, the devilment she would get into with her sisters, and moving to the big city of New York at age seven.

Without realizing it, my parents helped me to build images that included the concept that the world of being a Black child didn't begin and end with me. So in the third grade, when I heard stories about Tom Sawyer, I could see in my mind's eye my father having those same adventures. When I imagined myself as Scarlett O'Hara in *Gone with the Wind,* I was using the stories that my mother told me about the South. No, she wasn't raised on a plantation, but that didn't matter to me. She was a young woman, beautiful, had suitors, and survived hard times, and best of all she was Black like me.

These stories allowed me to build powerful images of myself as a young girl and as a woman. When we have powerful, competent images to draw on, we can continue to build on them.

> *How can we get these images? My mother never told me stories about her young life. It's not like we can go back to school and start over. Besides, going to school wasn't one of my all-time high points in life.*
>
> —*Flo*

Remember, we're never too old to learn. Reading and sharing experiences with other sisters help us to take in new information. There are a number of gifted Black women writers whose works can help us draw mental images of ourselves as competent and capable Black women; see the reading list at the back of this book.

Education can give us the basic concepts that help us to chart a better life for ourselves. In the recent past, education neglected to give us healthy, competent images of ourselves as Black women. The good news is that the educational systems of the present are changing. Today, schools are starting to include more multicultural learning. It's never too late to start something new. We can take a course in multicultural literature or in women's studies. We can also go to libraries and bookstores. Remember, our ability to learn is ongoing. We can go through the schoolhouse door as more-informed students and come out on the other side as powerful teachers.

9

▼▲▼▲▼

Taking the Time to Say Good-bye

Each year on my birthday I receive a phone call from my mother. "Well, kid, how does it feel to be almost grown?" is her customary greeting. "You mean to tell me I'm not there yet?" is my standard reply, and then we share a knowing laugh.

I've been married, given birth, divorced, acquired a mortgage, completed college, held several professional positions, and moved to another state. Yet in the eyes of my parents, I'll always be their child. In fact, the last time my mother visited me, we went for a walk, and she grabbed my hand as we prepared to cross a busy intersection. And to compound matters, my brothers and sister and I continue to call her Momi.

I sometimes get very caught up in my parents' view of me as a child needing protection and care. Then reality creeps in. The other day in the grocery store a young man (he was at least sixteen) addressed me as "ma'am," and I almost broke my neck trying to find the person he was addressing. By the time I discovered he was indeed talking to me, I was ready for some serious traction.

As comfortable as I am with my parents' need to see me as still a child, my age and life experiences confirm the reality that I'm an adult.

Actually, I'm grateful that my parents can see something I've apparently overlooked: the child in me. I've been an adult for so long that, for all intents and purposes, I sometimes believe I was born an adult, with high heels and lipstick intact. It's hard work being grown, and without my parents' sometimes humorous reminders (like the time I tried to bake a cake, and the dog wouldn't eat it), I do believe I might have forgotten to bid a healthy good-bye to my childhood years.

As Black women, our childhoods are often un-ceremoniously snatched away from us because of the demands of family survival. The care of younger brothers and sisters replaced Barbie dolls, and keeping house was not about playful fantasy. As children, we were given two messages: "be a child" (as in "you're not grown"), and "act like an adult" (as in "I want you to clean this kitchen and I want it spotless"). One message was direct—"be a child"; the other message was indirect—"act like an adult." While we heard the direct message, we were expected to act on the indirect message.

> *I always tell people that I chose not to have children because I wanted to pursue my career. But that's only half true. I was the third of ten and my mother worked, so I raised my seven brothers and sisters under me. I feel like I raised my children already and I just don't want to do that anymore.*
>
> *—Nettie*

The indirect message "act like an adult" was strong and the responsibilities were real.

> *I did everything for my younger sisters except breastfeed them, and I guess if I had breasts I would have had to do that too. In a way I'm still pretty overprotective of my sisters even though we're all grown.*
>
> *—Della*

Without fully understanding the seriousness of the adult tasks we were expected to perform, we filled shoes that were much too big for our small feet. Again, we didn't have a choice, and we weren't allowed to experience the full developmental process of girlhood.

In most respects, it's really not surprising to hear and read about the growing numbers of young teenage Black females who are mothers. If we're taught and expected to be mothers at an early age, chances are high that we will be mothers—not because we want to be parents, but because we've learned the role and its responsibilities at a tender age.

My parents were always after me as a child because they said I was acting grown. Most of the time I was grown, in spirit, if not in body.

—Angie

I envy my daughters their childhood. I'm making sure they have the childhood I never had.

—Jo

Once when my son's ten-year-old antics were grating on my last good nerve, I yelled out for him to act his age. Michael stopped for a split second to respond, "But I am acting my age. I'm ten, remember?" I had to laugh because of course he was right. We can learn from our children the merits of play.

I'm too old and much too tired to think about trying to be a child. As a matter of fact, I can't remember being a child, although I must have been one—how else would I explain being an adult?

—Tess

While it's true we can't turn back the clock and recapture what has been lost, we can become reacquainted with the part of ourselves that belongs to childhood. There's a song with the line "Step by step, each and every one of us travels down the road of life." I would change the lyric to say, "Stage by stage, each and every one of us moves down the road to adulthood." We weren't born adults, and taking on adult responsibilities as children, no matter how old we were at the time, didn't make us adults. We must pass through certain growth and developmental stages in order to become adults.

The only stages I remember passing are my birthdays, and when I reach thirty, I'm going to stop the clock.

—*Janet*

Birthdays are certainly one of the stage markers we use to show a form of life passage. But birthdays only show or mark our physical growth stage. Our emotional growth and development aren't as easy to track. Unlike physical growth and development, which are controlled by nature, our other forms of growth—emotional, mental, and spiritual—are nurtured and influenced by environmental forces such as family, church, school, and other types of social relationships. Nothing short of death at an early age interferes with our physical growth. However, our emotional, mental, and spiritual growth stages can be interrupted at any time. Generally, the interruptions are caused by severe trauma, like any form of abuse or witnessing or being involved in some type of tragedy.

But more often these three developmental stages of emotional, mental, and spiritual growth are interrupted in a more subtle way, such as when our feelings are continually ignored or dismissed, or when we are denied the experiences that enhance and nurture these parts of our growth. Being given responsibilities that were not age-appropriate and being expected to carry them out—sometimes without proper instruction on a continual basis—was an interruption to our developmental growth. We often don't miss these developmental stages of growth until we become adults and find ourselves in situations that require knowledge that we would have gained at these stages. Childhood experiences, such as having quality playtime or being allowed to try new and different things without the fear of being told we're wrong or stupid, give us permission to be creative and take risks as adults.

> *I can't say I miss my childhood. After mama died, I was in charge of the household and making sure the daily things got done. Playing was the last thing on my mind. But I don't think that it was bad for me to learn to be responsible when I was young. I mean being responsible got me through college, and it's a big part of my job.*
>
> —Maxie

While learning to be responsible is a major learning task in our lives, and learning it early puts us ahead of the game, learning the other life skills is equally important. There are a number of us who have a difficult time having fun or expressing how we think and feel about ourselves. We have a difficult time understanding ourselves as individuals because we've never had the opportunity to explore our total uniqueness.

Several years ago, at a conference, a woman asked who I was. Without a moment's hesitation, I rattled off my degrees, profession, and parental status. Before I could give my Social Security number, she politely interrupted me and explained that she was more interested in knowing me as an individual. Needless to say, her comment stopped me cold, because thinking of myself outside of my various adult roles meant reaching inside of myself and drawing on early life experiences and situations that helped to shape me as an adult.

In order to get to know myself as a more complete person outside of the various roles I played on a daily basis, I did the following exercise, which I would like to share with you. Give the exercise a try to see if you can discover any new information about yourself.

Find some childhood pictures of yourself; ask family members to contribute some from their collection. Now,

if your family is anything like mine, they've got a few photos stashed away for future blackmail purposes. If you can't find any pictures and your relatives refuse to part with theirs, thumb through some old magazines and cut out pictures of young girls that you believe resemble you at an early age.

Take your pictures to a quiet place and look at them. As you are looking at the pictures, remember the event that prompted the picture: was it a birthday, a holiday, a family gathering? Notice yourself in the pictures. How old were you at that time? What sort of things did you enjoy doing? Can you remember your favorite song, color, toys, friends? Look at the expression on your face. What does it look like you're thinking? Take the pictures and find a mirror. Look at the pictures and now look at yourself in the mirror. What's different? What's the same?

Some of my close women friends jokingly call me "Miz Thang," in reference to my sometimes cocky attitude. In looking at some of my childhood pictures, I discovered that several photographs revealed the same cocky (back then it was called "sassy") "don't mess with me" expression and posture that my friends recognize today. What I also recognize is that my cocky, sassy, "Miz Thang" attitude—which I choose to call firm determination—helps me to survive some rough times and it also helps me to laugh at myself.

Now I have come to love that little girl because she helped me to be the woman I am today. I could slowly move from the past, from my childhood, into my present womanhood with a sense of completion. It's my hope that, after doing this picture exercise, you will discover a little girl who is a part of the loving woman you've become.

PART THREE

▾▴▾▴▾▴▾▴▾

LORD, HOLD MY HAND WHILE I RUN THIS RACE

10

▼▲▼▲▼

Ain't Nobody Like My Baby

My friend Zoey falls in love three times a week and twice
on Sunday. I'm telling you, girlfriend, Zoey has been a
woman of the nineties since the seventies. This woman
takes no prisoners and holds no hostages. Zoey is real
clear about what she expects from a relationship, and
she'll tell you in a New York minute that she wasn't put on
this green earth to suffer at anyone else's expense, so at
the first sign of personal pain she'll drop a man like a bad
habit and keep right on stepping. Zoey's philosophy is
simple: love isn't supposed to hurt. And, given half a
chance, Zoey will tell you without a moment's hesitation
that in the department of love she has three major priorities: Me, Myself, and I.

My current significant friend truly respects and likes
not just women but all humankind, and it shows in his
interactions with others. He's considerate and kind and,
most of all, has a sense of humor about life and all its daily
craziness. He's able to be emotionally and physically supportive without being critical or believing that he's putting his manhood on the line. What I truly appreciate
about him is that he has solid basic values that shape his
life, but he doesn't inflict these values on others. No, he's
not perfect (a pot of beans without a ham hock floating in
the center borders on a capital crime in his book), but
perfect people don't exist on this planet. We're friends
because he has the characteristics I had in mind for someone special to share my life.

Now, while the majority of us don't possess my friend

Zoey's up-front, sassy, no-nonsense LWP (lust with potential) approach, or my criteria for selecting a significant friend, the sorry news is that in the partner-selection category, we tend to sell ourselves short. Everyone can't subscribe to Zoey's or my agenda for selecting a mate, but we can learn a lesson by examining some of the ins and outs of defining what will work for us in choosing the special someone to share our lives.

Let's take a look at our selection process. Now, while this is the decade of the nineties, and the emphasis for the past twenty-five years has been on women's personal empowerment, many of us sisters have held fast and steady to our childhood rule of if somebody likes you, then it's acceptable—no it's expected—that you like them back. Without really thinking about it, we often reflect the belief that it's somehow better to be chosen than to make the choice. Remember that fourth-grade game called "tag," where someone chased you down, tapped, slapped, or hit you on the nearest available body part, and then loudly proclaimed, "Tag, you're it." Many of our current partner-selection techniques resemble that fourth-grade game. While being chosen isn't a bad thing, we often find ourselves giving up much more than we originally bargained for in the tag department.

> *I don't wait to be chosen, I pick who I want to be with. But the problem is I always pick the wrong type of person.*
>
> —*Angie*

This remark is heard often, mainly from sisters who are experiencing problems in their relationships. While these sisters truly believe they've selected their partners, when they start examining the basic facts, it's not unusual to discover that tag was part of their experience too.

Okay, so what is a good indicator that we're playing tag instead of choosing someone to complement our life? Finding ourselves continually sacrificing our needs to meet the other person's wants should be the first red flag (indicator) to wave in our faces. When we find ourselves consistently altering or changing our values, beliefs, or personalities to please the other person, and—this is the important part—we're uncomfortable with the changes, sisters, there's something mighty wrong. Giving up what we believe in and losing our identities as individuals doesn't make for good relationships—it makes for nervous breakdowns. When we get that universal basic human instinct that som'thang ain't right, girlfriend, believe it, 'cause instincts don't lie.

> *Honey, if it hurts I'm history. Lov'n ain't supposed to hurt.*
>
> —Zoey

I would agree with Zoey that loving isn't suppose to hurt physically, emotionally, or spiritually, and if we're having any of these pains, it's time to consider our options. Having a clear idea of what we want in relationships will help us establish if we're choosing or being chosen. Knowing what we need in our lives gives us blueprints on which to build foundations. I can hear the questions now—well, hold tight, girlfriend, I'm fix'n to explain myself. When I was twelve years old, I used to daydream about how perfect my adult life would be. I would have a perfect loving husband, tons of lovely children, a perfect house, car, friends, and so on. Well, as an adult on my way to perfect, I got married, had a baby, bought a house, got divorced, kept the baby and the mortgage, got a job, completed college, got another job, got my son through high school and on his way to college, and guess what, I haven't reached perfect yet, catch my drift. My point is, we sometimes ride on our childhood dreams in making adult decisions. In order to make adult decisions, we have to be willing to ask ourselves grownup questions, because we're talk'n real life. A reporter once asked television personality Oprah Winfrey how she felt her boyfriend enhanced her life. Oprah, the total sister that she is, responded by stating that her boyfriend didn't enhance her life, he complemented it.

We can take a lesson from Oprah in asking ourselves "What type of partner would complement my life right now?" Am I ready to give and receive love versus do I need to be loved (hint: this is a tag question)? What things do I enjoy in another person? What can I bring to a relationship right now? What am I willing to give up to be in a relationship right now? Tough questions, you bet they are, but we're grownups, right? Having someone yell, "Yo! mama, I loves you," or some variation thereof, is not the basis on which satisfying, healthy relationships are formed. Zoey would say, "Having someone tell you they love you should be treated as a compliment not a commitment." Right on, Zoey.

While I'm in the right frame of mind, let's deal with that often misused, abused, and misunderstood "L" word. I'm talking the forever-and-ever-till-divorce-do-you-part word, not the Luther-Vandross-silk-sheets-hot-kisses "l" word—that's lust. I'm talking capital "L" word as in LOVE.

Would it surprise you to know that many sisters spend more time styling their hair than they do defining their concept of loving and being loved? Much too often the need for physical contact—the need to be held, the need for sex—masquerades itself in the comfortable disguise of love. Then we find ourselves caught in a web of emotional confusion. Not being able to define love for ourselves places us again in the position of depending on childhood rules in our adult world.

> *Mama told me not to give it up [have sex] until I found somebody I loved.*
>
> —*Flo*

> *I was told to keep my draw's up and my legs shut and don't bring nothing home that had to eat.*
>
> —*Bess*

Welcome to the wonderful world of adolescent sexual orientation of the fifties, sixties, and seventies. You may have heard a different version of these quotes depending on where you lived and who gave you the message, but it all adds up to sex isn't okay. The vast majority of us weren't given permission to see ourselves as sexual beings until love was declared as the winning reward. Growing up believing that we had to deny normal, healthy sexual needs unless someone convinced us that they loved us was bound to lead to adult confusion.

> *I grew up hearing that you'll know when it's really love. So at fifteen I thought I knew, and, bingo, my son was born the day after my sixteenth birthday.*
>
> *—LaTisha*

The final report on how to clarify one's definition of love is still out; however, there are a few basics that we can use for guidelines. Zoey refers to her guidelines as her shopping list. We can use any label that fits.

> *How can I have guidelines, when half the time I don't even know what I want the guy to look like?*
>
> *—Angie*

You can define for yourself what's physically acceptable to you. You can think about people you know or would like to know: What physical characteristics do they have that you admire? Go ahead, let your imagination run wild, and don't forget to add a few flaws—nobody's perfect. Next, define what qualities you want this person to have—throw everything into the pot. Now for the biggie. Image being next to this person, holding their hand. How do you feel, right now in the present? If what you're feeling is acceptable, then maybe you're close to what you want to experience in loving someone. Why the "maybe"? Well, the truth is no one can tell you how or what to feel—that's why the experts are still debating the issue. However, if what you're feeling is pleasurable, then it's acceptable. If, on the other hand, you experience any form of doubt, confusion, or fear, then—and I'm sure the experts would agree—you're not experiencing love. Why, you might ask yourself, would I experience doubt, confusion, or fear if I'm only imagining my ideal lover? The answer is that for some of us, even the thought of being with someone we would consider ideal plagues us with self-doubt ("Am I worthy?"), floods us with confusion ("Even in my imagination, he's too good for me"), and conjures up feelings of fear ("I'm afraid no one will want me"). Not all of us are ready for the "love thing," real or imaginary, even though we think we are ready.

Defining whom to love and how to love someone is as personal as the way you choose to wear your hair. And just as hairstyles come and go, your feelings and concepts of love will also change over the months or years.

We are led to believe that loving is like magic. It will cure all our ills, make our lives easier, and most of all make us more acceptable to everyone else. The truth is that we can only love someone else as deeply as we love ourselves. It's almost impossible to give someone something that we don't already have in our possession. How would we know if we were giving and receiving the genuine big "L" unless we had a reference point? True, the words "I've never felt this way before" sound good when we hear them in the movies, but that's Hollywood, not life. When we're clear about what love is for us, we can recognize when someone loves us. When we're not clear for ourselves, it becomes too easy to accept someone else's interpretation of love and loving, and that can often lead to big-time trouble. It's like Zoey says, lov'n ain't supposed to hurt, and she's right.

If someone says they love us and then disrespects us by hitting, calling us names, or withholding their affection, that's not love—that's abuse. And if you excuse these types of behaviors in the belief that what happened was motivated out of love, let me state again, love doesn't hurt. **People who share love don't intentionally hurt each other, through thought, word, deed, or action. Abuse of any kind on any level is unacceptable and dangerous.** There's a myth, no, I'll state it even stronger, there's a lie in our Black communities that advocates using violence on sisters, in the belief that we need to be kept in our place. The truth is no one has a place in the hands of violence. Sometimes we even want to hold ourselves responsible for our partners' abusive behavior toward us or others. This, my dear sisters, is impossible. Nothing you do can cause another person to act violently toward you. Only one person can decide how he will act, and that's the person who acts. We also have to be clear in understanding that we can't change a violent person's behavior by loving them enough. In all honesty, there isn't that much love in the world. This is not to say that we can't love people with violent behavior patterns. By all means, we can love them, because they need love too. But our choice to love them will not change their behavior. Remember, love isn't magic. The seductively sweet words "Baby, I'm sorry, it won't happen again" sound pleasingly loving when we're hurting, but please hear me and don't be deceived.

People who have violent behavior patterns need three things in order to change:

1. They have to *want* to change their behavior.
2. They must have *professional help* to learn more appropriate ways of handling their anger.
3. They need *encouragement* for learning new and different ways of behaving.

If loving enough could change abusive behavior, there wouldn't be any abusive people left on mother earth.

> *I don't really want a love thing right now, but I hate to give up the sex.*
>
> —*Cassie*

I used to believe that having sex with someone was loving them. Now maybe it's age, I don't know, but all sex does for me anymore is release tension. But I just can't go around having sex, or folks will think I'm cheap.
—Vy

Falling in love seems to make sex more acceptable for many of us, and while I don't want to knock a traditional belief, I've got a news flash for you. Wanting and having sex without the emotional attachment of love is perfectly acceptable. Now don't rush to the phone and call your mother on this one, 'cause she'll call my mama and I'll really be in trouble. The bottom line is that we're all sexual beings, and as sexual beings we experience certain needs. Men have known about emotionally detached sexual needs for years, and they've worked real hard to keep this secret among themselves.

It may sound amazingly incredible, but it's true. When it comes to the "physical thang," men appear to be much better at distinguishing "lust" from "love." These are two emotional lines that menfolk don't seem to have a problem keeping untangled. But then again, men have always had permission from society (this includes us women) to "sow their wild oats," while we as women have only had permission to "play tag." And while we are sitting patiently waiting for our phones to ring after that first initial "man meets woman" encounter, the fellows are generally hooking it up on another woman's line.

In fact, the first sexual act by a male is considered a guaranteed bona fide initiation into manhood. I once heard a male acquaintance proudly state about his five-year-old son, "I can't wait until my boy turns sixteen. I'm going to take him to his first 'cathouse' so the ladies can break him in, make him a man." Well, so much for emotional, loving attachments.

Yeah, but women who try to do all that sleeping around and other mess that men do get called nasty

names. Now I ain't got much else, but at least I got my
pride.

—*Angie*

Here's another news flash: having and enjoying close
personal relationships with men doesn't require being
sexual with them. We place unreasonably stringent limits
on ourselves if we choose to believe that the only relationships we can have with men are sexual. It's a myth that
"all men sleep around," and I can say this because I've
had the pleasure of meeting a lot of men who don't sleep
around. There are a number of men who would enjoy a
relationship with a woman without the pressure of thinking that they have to perform sexually.

If we allow men to believe that the only way they can
be close to us is through sex, then we end up playing tag
by their rules. This rule does not apply, however, if a man
physically or emotionally forces you to have sex. That
game is called sexual assault, and the rules here need to
include prosecution of the offender.

To be sexually active without the limits and bounda-
ries of "being in love" is a decision each woman can make
for herself. But as it is with most decisions, our emotional
agendas have to be clear. Having a clear emotional
agenda means that we have to be up-front with ourselves
(and hopefully with anyone we're choosing to be involved with) in asking ourselves the following questions:
Can I physically enjoy and be emotionally comfortable
having sexual activity without having stronger emotional
ties? Can I be honest with my sexual partner(s) about my
intentions? Am I willing to take responsibility for and
practice safe sex? How will I handle it if talk of my choosing to be sexual without commitment gets around? How
will I handle it if my partner wants more than I want to
give?

We also need to think about how we want to define
being sexual. Physical intercourse is only one definition,
and I might add that the choice of casual intercourse with-

out latex condoms isn't sexy—it's potentially deadly. Physical intercourse isn't everybody's cup of tea, but you don't have to give up the option of being sexual because you choose not to engage in intercourse. A wink, blink, and nod can be your definition of being sexual, if that's how you want to define sex. The bottom line is that we as women have choices regarding our sexual activity, and whatever we choose we must take responsibility for.

As far as people talking and calling us names—I can only speak for myself on this one—but my belief is that I don't suffer from guilt and shame when I make a personally responsible choice, so if some people don't like my choices and they choose to point their fingers and talk, I let them talk because, after all, I can only be directly responsible for the choices I've made. I can't be responsible for other people's assumptions about my choices.

Does all this stuff sound revolutionary? You bet it does! But let's be honest. We've been sexually active for years with and without commitment. All I'm pointing out is that we can take responsibility for our behavior and make conscious choices regarding our sexual activity. We don't have to wait to "fall in love" in order to fulfill our sexual needs, wants, and desires. We can base our need to be "in love" on other requirements, such as the person's being kind, easy to be with, fun to talk to, and sharing some of our other interests and goals in life.

Yes, indeedy, sweetie, men have been knowing this stuff for years. But this time somebody left the locker room door open and we've been listening. All those precious secrets are getting told. In all seriousness, being comfortable with being sexual is an important part of healthy self-esteem. There's no denying that most of us prefer a mutually loving relationship, but the reality is that for many reasons that's not always going to be the case.

Being sexually active is a major responsibility, and feeling good about your decision to have sex is your primary goal. While I can advocate sex without emotional attachments, I can't endorse unsafe sex. If you can't love the person you choose to be with, at least know the person well enough to enforce condom etiquette. Remember, your pleasure isn't worth your life.

Here's a little exercise that will help you to define your concept of love outside of a sexual framework. Take a pencil and paper and at the top write *Love is;* then go down the page listing all the things that represent your definition of love. You might be surprised to find that while there ain't nobody like your baby, there ain't nobody better to love than you.

11
▾▲▾▲▾
Women as Friends

For about a month after my divorce, all women known and unknown were the mortal enemy. The emotional wounds were deep and I wore my tearstained pride like a suit of armor. I wanted live prisoners to validate my declaration of war, to recapture what I believed to have been taken from me . . . my man. He was gone, being held an unwilling captive, or so I thought, in some other woman's arms, and as God is my witness, I was going to win him back!

I'm anxious by nature, so my mind worked overtime plotting, scheming, and praying (a childhood reflex), while my body followed along for the ride, losing sleep, weight, and energy. One afternoon, when I was just too tired to struggle, my friend Zoey, who had noticed my sudden cool distance and diminished state, took me to lunch. After listening to my tales of woe and plans of attack, she quietly said, "Girlfriend, I'm going to let you in on a big secret. You're hurting, but I'm not too worried about that 'cause you'll heal. But you're blaming the wrong folks for your pain. We sisters didn't do this to you. He's grown and he made his own decision, weak as it might be. We're not the enemy and neither are you. In fact, we can surround you and give you comfort if you let us." Zoey's sensitive and caring words didn't sink in right away, but as the days turned into months, she and a few chosen others, true to her words, helped me to move through my personal hell.

Over the years, I've heard similar versions of my experience from other sisters in deep personal pain. And I in turn shared Zoey's words of wisdom in the hope that somewhere along the line they would get the message that other sisters aren't the enemy. In truth, there isn't an enemy when someone we love chooses to move out of our life. But in all honesty the loss of love is not the only situation in which we want to hold another sister responsible for our personal grief.

We blame each other for a variety of personal dissatisfactions ranging from jobs to men. It's as if we believe that other sisters possess some magic—there's that word—that is more powerful than our own personal power.

From my own experience, I've developed a theory: **distrust is motivated by fear, and fear is motivated by the unknown.** My theory is based on the realization that today, when thinking about my loss, I recognize that I wasn't angry at the other women, I was angry at myself, because I didn't believe I could be who they were as women. I distrusted what I thought was their confidence, because I felt helpless; I feared their perceived strength because I felt weak. And most of all, I feared the unknown certainty of my future. Over the years, I've watched this theory played out again and again by sisters who distrust and fear the unknown qualities of other sisters.

> *I was taught not to trust other Black women, because if they get too close they want something you've got.*
> —*Flo*

In my talks with other sisters, I've found Flo's experience to be a common one. It's as if our individual beliefs concerning our personal inadequacies are projected onto others. We try to hold other sisters hostage in the hopes of ignoring our own personal pain.

> *I purposely chose to attend an all-Black college in the hopes of finding and developing a closer bond with other Black women. Honey, was I ever in for a shock.*

Half the sisters on campus wouldn't even talk to me. Later on my roommate told me it was because they thought my fair complexion and straight hair meant that I was stuck on myself. They didn't even try to get to know me. It's as if they blame me for being born. I didn't have any say about how I came into the world.

—Jo

My ex-boyfriend's mother told me that it was okay to date her son, but not to set my heart on marrying him 'cause bloodline was important in their family. When I asked him later what she meant, he said that he was really catching it from her because she thought I was too dark.

—Nettie

Sad, but true: as long as we allow such things as physical features, education, and economic class to become issues that divide us, there can never be unity among us. Having absorbed so many painful, negative messages about Black women, we can be immune to the pain we inflict when we verbally scorn our sisters. Because we have been so devalued for so many generations, we feel threatened by the reflection of ourselves in others. We can only honor, respect, and accept the beauty in others when we accept those things in ourselves.

Now, am I saying we must love and like all Black women? No. It's unrealistic to think that we have to like everyone; however, it's important that we know and understand why we dislike the sister. If our dislike is based on superficial reasons, things like the coloring of her hair, skin, nails, her body structure, or her life-style, then we might want to check our own backyard, as my mama would say. When dislike of another person is based on these types of characteristics, there's a good chance that we're playing the internal comparison game. The next time we find ourselves disliking a sister, we need to stand quiet and still for a minute and listen to our thoughts, that internal private self-talk that everyone engages in from time to time. What are we saying to ourselves? If we find ourselves making accusatory statements or questions about the other woman, such as "She must think she's cute . . . ," or "Who does she think she is?" then chances are good that we're playing the comparison game. When we notice the cue, we can quietly give ourselves the internal message "I'm okay just as I am." We then need to pay close attention to how we feel after giving ourselves that message. Generally, when we dislike a person based on the comparison game, there is a good chance that we're feeling personally threatened on some level. By giving ourselves the internal message that we're okay as we are, we allow the threatening feeling to pass out of our awareness.

Our choice to dislike someone needs to be as clear and honest as our choice to like someone else. It's honest to dislike someone if she is offensive, abusive, dishonest, or in some way disrespects our sense of personal values. I personally have a strong dislike of anyone—be it sister, brother, or anyone else—who knowingly abuses children in any way, shape, or form. The act of child abuse offends my values and beliefs about the sacredness of children.

Getting to know, respect, and appreciate the diversity and individuality of other sisters can only bring us closer to honoring those traits within ourselves.

12

▼▲▼▲▼

Mad Love Affair

I love myself when I'm laughing.

—Zora Neale Hurston

I'm having a mad love affair, and ohhhh wieee baby is it hot. I get flowers, dine in the best places, see the number one shows, and the lov'n is fantastic. I'm saying, girl-friend, I'm having the time of my life with the person of my life.

Since you're dying to know just who the lucky person is, and I'm dying to tell my business . . . the lucky person giving and receiving all my attention these days is Me. That's right—Me!! I'm having a mad love affair with my-self. Am I crazy? Maybe. Am I happy? Most of the time. Am I lonely? Sometimes. Am I sorry? Never. No, I'm not conceited, I'm just convinced that I'm worth loving, and who can do a better job of loving me than me? Loving me doesn't exclude my loving others, it just means I've put myself at the top of the list of those I choose to love.

Throughout this book, I state that "Somewhere be-tween selfish and selfless is self-care." Having a mad love affair with ourselves is first-rate self-care.

I don't know, loving yourself sounds kind of silly to me. I know I should, but just how do you learn to love yourself?

—Tess

Our problem is not learning to love ourselves, but learning to show how much we love ourselves. We get so caught up in waiting and wanting someone else to love us that we forget how to give this good stuff to ourselves.

Think about it. When's the last time you've given yourself flowers? Bought a lavish gift just for you? Treated yourself to a good movie or show? Or taken a first-rate vacation just for yourself? When's the last time you've looked yourself square in the eye (using a mirror, of course) and said, "I love you, with all of your imperfections and faults"? The serious truth is we don't do these things for ourselves, yet we'll do these things and much more for someone else. We'll take the time and energy to give our Mr. Rights (who often turn out to be Mr. Wrongs) the sun, moon, and stars, yet we'll neglect to give ourselves a fifteen-dollar bouquet of flowers. And to put the icing on the cake, if Mr. What's-His-Name forgets or neglects to return our show of affection, we blame and criticize ourselves for not being good enough.

> *I can do those things for myself, but it just feels special when someone does them for me.*
> —*Janet*

We count on others to recognize and acknowledge our specialness. But how can we expect others to acknowledge something we neglect? We reflect what we feel. When we take care of ourselves, by treating ourselves special, we show our value to the world.

> *But isn't that faking it? Sure, I can give myself flowers and tell myself I love me, but it doesn't last long. It just seems like the real thing when someone does it for you.*
> —*Nettie*

As Zoey pointed out to me not too long ago, "Nothing is forever except death and taxes." And lov'n is no exception to this rule. Sure, giving ourselves compliments or gifts may not seem real in the beginning, but it's only because we're new at these things. Even when we're in a relationship, we don't hear "I love you" or receive gifts every day. When we do these things for ourselves, we have the option of doing them daily or once in a while.

We've been conditioned by society to believe that doing good things for ourselves is selfish. Actually, when we examine the total picture, we come out on the self-denying end of the scale. By neglecting to pay attention to ourselves, by being selfless, we suffer the deprived, empty feelings of loneliness. Emotional deprivation is first cousin to emotional neediness, and let me tell you, girlfriend, emotional neediness shines like a hundred-watt lightbulb. We grow old, hard, and cold storing up all of our lov'n for that special someone who may or may not come along.

> When you talk about lov'n, I know what you mean, but when I think about lov'n, I think about do'n the do. You know, the physical thang.
>
> —Cassie

Doing the do or the physical thang is very much a part of loving ourselves. Okay, I'm going to break a traditional Black community taboo and talk about masturbation, or as I like to call it, self-pleasuring, the act of sexual self-gratification.

Self-pleasuring is the ultimate form of self-care and self-love.

> I was always taught that playing with myself, or touching myself was wrong. It was dirty.
>
> —Vy

Contrary to popular belief and age-old myths, there is nothing wrong or dirty about touching our bodies. We touch ourselves all the time. When we go to the bathroom, when we wash and clothe ourselves, we are touching our bodies. Isn't it amazing that we're never hesitant to sexually stimulate men's genitals in the act of loving them, but we stop short of giving ourselves this very same kind of love. It does make one wonder how it is that we can ask our vaginas to be best friends with men's penises when we neglect a friendship with that part of ourselves? If it's acceptable for men to touch us sexually, then why deny ourselves the same pleasure?

Loving isn't just about a physical thing; the absence of intercourse doesn't mean we're not sexual, and it doesn't mean we're not lovable. Loving ourselves is a total integration of mind and body.

I always thought that you had to love yourself on the inside first.
—*Tess*

There isn't concrete evidence that proves we have to love ourselves a certain way. There is a lot of literature that supports the belief that one needs to have a certain level of self-acceptance to have a healthy life. However, the ways in which we acquire and maintain self-acceptance are clearly linked to the ways in which we care for ourselves. By giving ourselves compliments and gifts, we show that we value our individual selves. It never fails when I take the time to dress special or do something special for myself, I start to feel special. And when I feel special, that feeling generates outward and affects my surroundings. Talk about a powerful feeling—feeling special is ultimate power.

Come on, girlfriends, let's have a mad love affair with ourselves. Let's buy flowers, treat ourselves to fine meals, take in some shows, put on our sexy nighties, and whisper daring sweet nothings in our own ears. Here are some tips on how to create your own mad love affair:

- Buy yourself a single red rose.
- Go to an upscale department store. Find the designer section and try on all the latest fashions.
- Dress in your finest and take yourself to lunch or dinner.
- Write yourself a love poem.
- Buy a book on self-pleasuring (check out the women's section of most bookstores). Take a nice warm scented bath, put on your favorite oils, snuggle under the covers, and read. If you feel brave enough, try some of the exercises in the book. If you don't feel brave, just relax in the comfort of feeling loved by the person who counts most—*You*.

13

▼▲▼▲

Sexual Heal'n

ZOEY: Sis, we got't talk.

ME: Yeah, Zoey, what's up?

ZOEY: Well, I don't mean to be tell'n you your business, but something's miss'n in those last three chapters.

ME: Well, let's see, I talked about partner selection, friendships between women, and self-love. What did I leave out?

ZOEY: Seems to me that a whole lot of us sisters are get'n trashed on the homefront because of who we love and how we love them. I think something major needs to be said.

ME: I hear you loud and clear, Zoey. Thanks for the tip.

ZOEY: You're welcome. That's what I'm here for, sweet-cakes.

Well, Zoey has brought me to the mark again. Her point is well taken, because sex is important, and validating our sexual needs, wants, and desires is a major part of self-acceptance.

As Black women, we've been sexually oppressed for years. There has been more said about our sexuality than about that of any other race of women on God's green earth. Our sexuality has been stereotyped: "Black women are hot lovers"; categorized: "Black women are great lovers"; mystified: "Black women are oversexed"; and dehumanized: "Black women are animals in bed." But rarely are we allowed to experience our sexuality for what it truly is—a normal part of our human biological makeup.

For years, we've been oppressed by these sexual stereotypes and myths. Unfortunately, these oppressive messages have reached our ears, minds, bodies, and souls, and have taken their toll on us. In trying to reach the utopian middle ground of accepting and enjoying our sexuality, some of us have landed somewhere on the extreme ends of the sexual continuum. Either we deny our sexuality or we play out the totally stereotyped Black sexual myth. Being on either end of the continuum is uncomfortable and not very realistic in terms of having healthy self-esteem.

> Say some more about this sexual continuum stuff. I'm not sure I get what you're say'n.
>
> —Angie

Our Black communities tend to be pretty rigid in terms of sexuality and women. We're given unspoken but strict social messages about what's considered proper in terms of appropriate sexual behavior. On one side of the continuum, we have messages like "Don't have sex without the benefit of marriage." The message: deny your sexual self. On the other side of the continuum, we have messages like "Being too sexual is indecent." The message: being sexual is wrong. The continuum is negative at both ends, and the strict social laws of the community leave us very little room for flexibility in the middle. Somewhere in between these two positions we have sisters who are struggling to find a range of comfort for themselves sexually. In other words, we're doing what we believe is socially and sexually acceptable.

The miracle and gift of being born women is a testament to our given right to enjoy and take pleasure in our sexuality. Being able to take pleasure in expressing ourselves sexually means that we value and take pride in who we are as women.

The art of sexual expression has as many variations as ice cream has flavors. To put it plainly, sexuality has a wide range of expression. And within that range of expression, we notice ourselves being attracted to individuals who will fulfill our needs. Some of us are attracted to men, some of us are attracted to women, and some of us are attracted to men and women.

Wait! Hold on just a minute here. I was with you until you said being sexually attracted to women. Now talk'n about loving another sister is one thing, but when you start talk'n about sisters being sexual with each other, well, that's somethin' else. Two women having sex together just ain't natural. And that mess about being sexually attracted to men and women is just plain crazy.

—Della

Our attitudes and beliefs about women being sexual with each other is what's unnatural, not the women who express their natural sexuality in that manner.

I always knew I loved women, but I knew it wasn't safe to act on this awareness, 'cause my family just couldn't handle it. While I was trying to make the decision about coming out, I got so depressed my doctor put me in the hospital for two weeks. My family thought I was working too hard. But I knew that coming out meant giving up not only my family, but my friends, church, and community as well. I guess that's why I moved so far away. I figured it was easier to move halfway across the States than give up people I loved.

—Cassie

I came out to my mother last night. She told me that I was sin'n against God, and until I got myself right I wasn't welcome in her house.

—Cassie

Cassie is being oppressed because she shared her sexual identity with her mother. Choosing not to hide or ignore her sexuality put her in the position of being judged by her mother, who decided she was unworthy of acceptance. Mom made a judgment based on her belief about God. But I believe that it was Mom's beliefs, not God's, that made her turn her daughter away.

As far as sisters being bisexual, sometimes it's more a choice born out of safety then natural sexual attraction to men.

Lov'n another woman ain't never been safe on the homefront. And I ought to know, 'cause I stayed married to a man for twenty years and had five kids, but I've always been more attracted to women. I used to hear folks talk about women lov'n women, call'n us names and such, and it was ugly. Well, my husband's been dead for five years, and I been with Pauline for three years now, and my life ain't never been so good. I guess I'm just at an age now where I don't give a damn what nobody says.

—Bess

Cassie and Bess are both the victims of the extreme tension that exists in the Black community concerning our lack of freedom in sexual expression. Again, the unspoken, rigid code of sexual conduct places us in the position of having to hide a part of ourselves in order to be "socially acceptable" to the community and outside world. The world would be such a nice, neat, tidy place if we were all alike and did everything, and I do mean everything, in the same way. But I've got a serious news flash. Nobody knows better than we do that nothing in the world is that simple. Imposed silence of any kind is deadly and hurts us all. When we choose to ignore or degrade another sister based on her sexual identity, we all feel the pain. Our sexual needs and desires are all different, and being different doesn't make them wrong.

> *Well, it may not be simple, and Lord knows it's different, but it ain't right, even says so in the Bible.*
> —*Della*

I'm no expert on the Bible so I can't quote it chapter and verse, but I do know that the main message of the Bible is to love and accept each other, and it doesn't make exclusions based on gender, race, creed, or sexuality, though some people do interpret it that way, for reasons of their own. Our Black lesbian and bisexual sisters are sisters without cause or exception and deserve the same honor and respect that we all deserve. When we place ourselves in a position of judgment, then we turn ourselves into oppressors. Healthy self-esteem cannot exist side-by-side with oppression of any kind.

> *I'm with you, sis. Seems to me that God's got a whole lot more important things to do than worry about who we're having sex with.*
> —*Zoey*

> *Well, you all can say what you want, but I heard that having all these gay people sleep with each other is the reason everybody's get'n AIDS.*
> —*Flo*

Experts in the health field tell us that heterosexuals (that's clinical language for straight folks) stand the greatest risk of getting AIDS by doing three things: (1) having unsafe sex with numerous partners; (2) using unclean IV (intravenous) drug needles; or (3) having sex with a person who has AIDS or is an IV drug user. In that respect, we straight women are at a greater risk of getting AIDS than lesbian sisters. (Of course, lesbians and bisexual women need to practice safe sex too.) There is also new evidence that shows that heterosexual teenagers are the fastest-growing population of people who are turning up HIV positive and developing AIDS. And we also have the dilemma of gay brothers, who feel forced to hide their sexual identity within the community, dating and marrying sisters while continuing to be sexual with men. But the point I want to make here is we don't get AIDS from gay or lesbian people. We get AIDS by making unsafe sexual choices. And if you're having sex without latex condoms, then you're at high risk.

> *Personally, I don't really care who sisters share their beds with, but I can't say that I like seeing them being so public with one another.*
>
> —*Maxie*

I need to say this again, because it's a very important point: it's not our place to pass judgment on anyone because of her sexual life-style. As members of the African-American race, we've all shared the shackles of life-style oppression for too many years. It's time to break those chains, and it can begin with us as sisters accepting and respecting each other and our expressions of our differences.

Speaking for myself, when I see two sisters loving and caring about each other, regardless of their sexuality, I see the ultimate extension and reflection of my own sense of self-love. When we truly love and care about ourselves, it's a real natural progression to extend our love to others. I find any outward sign of that love beautiful.

ZOEY: Say, sis . . .

ME: Okay, Zoey, what did I leave out this time?

ZOEY: No, sis, you're doing fine. It just sounds like you're get'n ready to close the chapter. And I was wondering if you could do me a favor, is all.

ME: Sure, if I can. What is it?

ZOEY: Could you say somethin' about hav'n partners of other races? I think we need to hear something about this too.

JANET: I'm sure glad Zoey brought that up, 'cause I get tired of feeling like I'm some kind of traitor every time I'm out with my white boyfriend. I mean I get some wicked stares whenever we're out together. My own sister had the nerve to tell me that I wasn't comfortable being Black, cause if I was then I'd date Black men.

Our sexual attractions cover a wide range of choices. Any sexual choices we make—provided those choices aren't dangerous or abusive to ourselves or others—are the right choices for us. It's just as acceptable to love and be sexual with a person of another race as it is to be loving and sexual with someone of the same race. Healthy self-esteem is not based on the color or sex of our sexual partners; it's based on the belief that we respect our rights and the rights of others to make personal choices.

Interracial dating and marriage have always been a part of our community. Brothers have done it for years.

Well, just because brothers do it, that don't make it right. It's up to us sisters to set an example of united Blackness. If sisters start dating and marrying out of the race, what will happen to Black families?

—*Jo*

Sisters, like brothers, who choose to date or marry interracially are expressing their choice of sexual freedom.

Again, there aren't any right or wrong ways (as long as they are safe) to express a sexual choice. We will remain Black no matter what choices we make, and the last time I checked there weren't any honest ways of measuring a person's ethnicity. It's funny, I've never heard a person in an interracial relationship express concern, doubt, or worry about their racial identity. And this leads me to believe that they're not the insecure ones—get my point?

As far as Black families are concerned, there have always been Black families, and there will always be Black families. Interracial relationships aren't a threat to our lineage or heritage—they're an enhancement. I'm convinced that Black mixed with any color still shines through just as pretty.

For years, sisters have been made to feel totally responsible for the unity of our race. We have taken on the task without questions or doubt, only to be given little credit or recognition for a job well done. I'm of the belief that we are not—and cannot continue to view ourselves as—the glue that holds the race together. The job is much too big. When we buy into the myth that we alone are responsible for an entire race of people, we place ourselves in the position of believing that we're superhumans. This line of thinking also discredits the numerous contributions that Black men have made to our cultural survival.

> *Even if all those things you say are true, I still don't like to see sisters be with men from other races.*
>
> —Vy

It's okay not to like it, but we need to remember that our personal discomfort with a sister's sexual choice doesn't make her choice disappear. We can save ourselves a lot of mental anguish if, instead, we decide to openly respect the person's right to make the choice. We're individuals and our individual differences make us stronger as sisters.

Being able to love and accept our individual sexual preferences without the fear of being disrespected by others allows us to openly love ourselves that much more.

After all, healthy sexual acceptance is a major part of healthy self-esteem, so let's get down with some sexual heal'n.

14

▼▲▼▲▼

Body Talk

At the root of every Black woman's illness is
disappointment and sorrow.

—Overheard at the National Black Women's Health
Project Conference, Seattle, 1986

I just returned from visiting my friend Sharon in the
hospital. Two days ago, Sharon had half of her stomach
and large intestine removed. Cancer.

"How ya doing, hon?" I asked as I looked at her tiny
nut-brown body propped up by a mountain of snow-
white pillows.

"Well, girlfriend, I guess this poor old body finally said
all the things I couldn't let my mouth say." As I took her
hand in a gesture of comfort, we both began to cry.

At forty-three, Sharon, a single mom to four teenagers
and a nurse's aide at a local hospital, had spoken for all of
us. Her body had given away the secrets she had worked
so hard to keep.

I once heard someone say that if you want something
to be secret don't tell a Black woman. What a joke! We're
the best secret keepers on God's green earth. Yeah, we
gossip, but never about the things that count—ourselves.
We keep our emotional hurts carefully locked and hidden
within our physical selves. Believing the myth that silence is strength, we're letting our emotional pains slowly
kill us, bit by bit.

I don't know about you, but I wasn't raised to put my personal business in the street.

—Janet

Pardon me a minute, while I put on my Miz Thang hat, 'cause I get a serious attitude when it comes to this topic.

From my position as a clinical psychotherapist who works in a medical setting, I would estimate that about six out of every ten Black women in this country suffer from some type of major physical disorder related to their emotional well-being. Pay attention, ladies, there isn't a neat, polite, professional way to say it: we're dying in large numbers from physical ailments that are linked to emotional stresses. Our silence isn't golden, it's deadly.

We're using drugs, alcohol, self-starvation, overeating, and careless sexual choices as a means of comfort to quiet our emotional hurts. But these methods of comfort aren't working for us, they're working against us. Physical health problems such as obesity, anorexia, hypertension, heart disease, diabetes, headaches, various forms of cancer, alcoholism, and HIV/AIDS are your body's way of saying, "Look'a here, girlfriend, you can keep your mouth shut if you want, but I'm about to tell all your business." Our bodies are literally sick of our imposed silence, and they are physically doing the talking for us.

I always thought that taking care of my body was my own business. Besides, when I'm sick, I go to the doctor.

—Maxie

Our bodies are our personal business, but recent health reports confirm that we haven't been taking care of business. True, it's always been more acceptable in the Black community to seek medical help as opposed to other types of help. But often we ignore the emotional signals that we're hurting, so by the time we do seek medical attention, what might have been a minor problem has blown into a major medical problem. We've learned to self-medicate with food, drugs, alcohol, and sex, as a means to build up our tolerance of pain and bypass our emotional hurts.

The other issue here is skyrocketing medical costs. In plain language, this means that very soon illness is going to be a luxury that we won't be able to afford.

> *I don't know, sis. I'm having a hard time digesting what you're say'n. Six out of every ten Black women suffering seems pretty high to me. Making a connection between all those types of physical problems and emotional problems seems pretty farfetched. And even if what you're say'n is so, we can't cure cancer and everything else just by talk'n about it.*
>
> —Flo

To paraphrase the words of the National Black Women's Health Project founder, Byllye Y. Avery, I'm not interested in what you believe—what do the facts say? Pain, illness, and death aren't beliefs, they're facts, and the facts are coming from the most credible sources—you and I and every other Black woman who has set foot in a hospital emergency room or doctor's office seeking help. The daily stresses of working outside of the home, caring for children, managing a home, and paying bills put a lot of emotional and physical pressure on our minds and bodies. Most of the time, we don't give it a second thought when we miss a meal or get an ache or pain. "I'll take care of it later" is usually what we think, but later never seems to come. Before we know it, we're sitting in a doctor's office because our problem has gotten so bad we can't ignore it. Pain of any kind never has been and never will be a totally personal issue where Black women are concerned. When we're hurting, our pain affects those around us—our children, lovers, husbands, friends. When we become immobilized with emotional or physical pain, we often make unwise choices in an effort to find relief.

I'm a prime example of this one. Two years ago I had to have a partial hysterectomy because I was too busy with "other" things. I had a job to do, meetings to attend, a child to raise, workshops to conduct . . . Sure, I noticed the cramping, and yeah, my monthly menses were becoming heavier and lasting longer. "But hey," I reasoned to myself, "this is what aging is all about." Wrong answer! My body was trying in no uncertain terms to tell my thick head something was wrong. Well, I finally got the message and the courage to talk to my doctor about the problem, but only after the most embarrassing situation in my life occurred. Okay, I won't keep you in suspense. I knocked over my large purse at the counter in the checkout line at Safeway, and six super loooong maxipads spilled out on the counter in front of God and everybody else in the line. It was as if my unconscious mind was saying, "Okay, girlfriend, if you won't pay attention to all the other signs that something's not right with our body, then I'll really give you a clue and bam!!" Remember, I said before there are no accidents in the universe, and I like to think of this incident as the goddess's way of telling me to take some action. I talked to my mother (I always check out medical problems with Momi first), and she assured me that severe cramps and three menstrual flows a month weren't part of the aging process. By the time I saw my doctor, the fibroid tumors had grown so large that my uterus couldn't be saved. Luckily, my ovaries could be spared. When my doctor asked if I had been in pain, I honestly answered, "Yes, but the pain would go away," and "I always had plenty of supplies to handle the flow." When she asked why I hadn't come in sooner, my only response was "I didn't have time." Wrong answer, she said. "When your body tells you something, you better start paying attention—that is, if you want to keep your body in one piece." All I can say is I've learned my lesson. Choosing to ignore my physical pain and emotional distress by being "too busy" to pay attention wasn't wise.

Talking to someone doesn't cure physical problems,

but it can relieve the stress. By talking to my mother and a few other friends who, as it turns out, had had similar problems, I could have gotten important information. Our minds and bodies aren't separate—what affects one directly affects the other. No, talking won't cure cancer or a lot of other physical problems, but maybe talking will relieve some of the built-up emotional and mental stresses on our minds that can make our bodies more vulnerable to cancer and other physical ailments.

Who do we talk to? Most of the people I know have their own troubles and don't want to be bothered with mine.

—Jo

Talk to someone you trust: a minister, therapist, counselor, teacher, or good friend. Talking is only half the solution, but it's important. When we talk to someone, our emotional vision clears and we get needed information to relieve the stress. Then we can take some form of action.

Taking action is the half of the solution that is directly linked to prevention. Here's what I mean: **Taking action might mean changing food habits, such as eating in a healthy way to cut down on the risk of heart disease and stomach problems. When we don't have to worry about our hearts and stomach hurting, we can take care of other business.**

Calling and talking to a friend about the crazy day on the job relieves stress just as well as having a drink. Taking some strenuous physical action, like walking, jogging, working out, or other body exercises, is a good stress-buster too. There is some truth to the cause and effect theory where our bodies are concerned, but we have to be willing to listen to what our minds and bodies are telling us. Remember, we've got young sisters out there depending on us to show them the way. We can let our healthy bodies do some of the talking for us.

15

▼▲▼▲▼

Show Me the Way

The thing I believe. God is inside you and inside
everybody else. You come into the world with God.

—Alice Walker, *The Color Purple*

When I think about my relationship with God, I think
about shoes. Now for those of you who don't know me,
this sounds strange, and for those of you who do know me,
this still sounds strange—but then you also know I've always been a wee bit strange but credible in my own fashion. The truth is I love God and I love shoes, and I'm
willing to say more on the subject, but I need to be up-
front in saying that I had some serious doubts about including this chapter. My doubts centered around the
thought that talking to others about something as personal and private as a relationship with God is scary business. But Zoey convinced me to keep this chapter when
she told me, "Something needs to be said. How can you
talk to us about having healthy self-esteem and good relationships with ourselves, if you leave out what's important to us—our relationship with God?"

Zoey was right, of course. I'm telling you, that woman
has the best track record of anybody I know for being
right on the money. When I thought about what I wanted
to say and how to say it, girlfriend came to the rescue
again with "Just tell your truth and the rest will take care
of itself." So with Zoey's support, here's my truth.

When something frightens me, I search for a way to

make it less frightening and more familiar. Talking about my relationship with God frightens me because my belief is something very personal and still very much in its evolutionary stage. Talking about my relationship with shoes is more familiar. Honey! I can spot good leather a mile away, and I'm always willing to share the merits of a great buy. On the other hand, talking about my relationship with God, well, about all I can say is pull up a chair and an open mind.

Actually, my thoughts about God and shoes have some interesting parallels.

When I spot a great pair of shoes in a boutique window, I can't resist the urge to try them on. Now when I was younger the need to look cute often overrode my common sense regarding size. So I would wind up buying shoes that didn't quite fit, but I was cute for as long as I could keep those shoes on my feet. Let me tell you, I had a closet full of shoes that spent more time off my feet than on. As I got older I discovered that the money it took to relieve my corns, calluses, and bunions was putting a serious dent in my shoe-buying money. I also discovered that no matter how cute those shoes were, limping just wasn't sexy.

Now I know you're asking, how does all this talk about shoes relate to a relationship with God? Well, I was just coming to that part.

When I was younger, I wore my relationship with God like my cutest pair of shoes. I was proud of what I had and wanted everyone to see it. I was so devout that the reflection from the halo would send shivers down your spine. You know the program, church every Sunday, and on holy days, memorizing the gospel, weekly catechism, reading the Bible—we're talk'n heavy church pride. I was a strong believer without question or doubt.

Then something happened—my divorce to be specific—and my view of the world, based on my religious beliefs about God, collapsed. I was devastated, frightened, and alone. How? Why? What had I done to cause

God to punish me in such a fashion? Not only was I abandoned by my husband, but God was deserting me too. In desperation, I attended church daily, searching for answers, clues, and forgiveness, but always in my efforts I came away empty, lonely, and generally with more questions than answers. After a number of months, my hurt and grief turned to anger. If my religion could turn its back on me, I could do likewise, and into the back of the closet went my religion and belief in God.

My son, then seven years old, having gone through the trauma of divorce and forced to live with my hectic work and school schedule, developed a serious case of asthma. As I was racing him to the hospital at three in the morning, during one of his more severe attacks, I heard myself bargaining out loud with the Almighty. "God, you've just got to save my little boy's life, he's all I got left. I'll go back to church, I'll do whatever you want, just save my son."

The emergency room team was ready and waiting when we arrived. They worked several long hours to bring Michael a measure of comfort and relief. "Okay God, if this was a test, you win. You kept your part of the bargain and I'll keep mine." I returned to church that following Sunday, but it was as if I had a chip on my shoulder. My body was present, but my mind wandered effortlessly as I numbly watched the priest perform the offertory. "The fit isn't right," I told myself, feeling empty after the third Sunday of attending mass. The next week I tried a different religious institution, only to find myself again kicking off the service like ill-fitting shoes. This process of attending various religious services, in an effort to keep my commitment to God, continued for several months. "Okay God, if you want me back, you better do something quick. I'm not willing to keep going through this," I muttered out loud as I was driving home after yet another failed attempt. In discussing my religious dilemma with Zoey, who is, as we know, pretty right on the money, I was able to make a very important discovery, one that changed my life. Our conversation went like this:

ZOEY: Who were you talk'n to in the car at three A.M.?

ME: I told you, Zoey, God.

ZOEY: And who were you talk'n to in the car on Sunday?

ME: God. It was God both times.

ZOEY: I rest my case.

ME: Come on, Zoey, it can't be that simple.

ZOEY: Why can't it?

ME: Well, I don't know, but it just can't be.

ZOEY: Says who?

ME: Well, I don't know, but I made a promise to go back to church and come back to God.

ZOEY: From those conversations, and all the church hop'n you been doing, sounds to me like you kept your end of the deal.

ME: I don't know, Zoey.

ZOEY: Listen up, sweetcakes. [She always gets a little testy when I don't get the message right off.] God don't need a lot of fancy wrap'n, that was your idea. God is go'n be wherever you are. If you need a church or religion in order to be with God, then I suggest you keep on searching. But it looks to me like God never left you.

With this conversation, my search for religion ended and my new relationship with God began. In her great wisdom, Zoey had helped me discover that it was the traditional formal constraints of religion that didn't fit, not God. I wanted and found that God could be with me without the tight squeezing and pinching of a wrong fit. The more I discovered and embraced my new form of spirituality, the more I enjoyed the wonders of God within and around me. I was also able to understand why my search for religion left me feeling pinched and squeezed.

As a Black woman who grew up in a devout Catholic home with a liberal dose of good old-fashioned down-home Southern Baptist values tossed in for good measure, I discovered that my former religious training had me locked into a codependent relationship with God.

Now don't get mad and close the book. Hear me out first. Remember, I said in the beginning that this chapter was scary business, but I was willing to take the risk, so stick with me because there might be some information here for you too.

Religion plays an important role in our lives as Black women. It helps us to define our personal morals and gives us a code of conduct for choosing how to live day to day. When we say we are religious, we generally mean that we worship and believe in a traditional formal structure that includes a hierarchy with God at the top. The rest of the hierarchy is generally composed of "men" in the middle and women and children on the bottom. The way that most traditional religions are structured, men have been responsible for our interpretation and concept of how we worship and view God. As Black women who have learned and practiced religion based on a hierarchy that's been constructed from a male perspective, we've been seriously shortchanged. The male perspective of worshipping God ignores our inherent "womanness." The standard practices of religious worship would have us believe that God is an authoritarian master who sits in punitive judgment of our daily lives in much the same way that a tyrannical father would. This belief is fostered through the various roles we are required to play within the religious structure, such as "Mothers or sisters of the church." This puts us in service to others but rarely gives us direct leadership, fostering the belief in male superiority. True, we are now "taking" more direct roles, but notice these roles aren't given freely and, as such, our leadership as ministers is still questioned and scrutinized by many who feel it is not a woman's place to lead others.

We are also required to follow special rules such as how to dress and conduct ourselves and our families in order to meet the requirements of being true believers. These rules are meant to keep us in "our place" as female servants of man, i.e., God. In a more subtle manner, we are even told how to think: God is to be given credit for all that is good in our lives, whereas we are directly responsible for all that goes wrong. If something "bad" happens, we are directed to pray for forgiveness because surely we must have displeased God in some way.

I believe that this form of traditional religion was never part of God's plan—but rather is man's concept of how religion should be viewed. Worshipping God is not about religion—"the package that is imposed on God"—but more about the reality of knowing ourselves and discovering God through ourselves. I believe that all living matter is a creation and representation of God's divine love. Therefore I believe that we are all God and God is all of us. Cecil Williams, the pastor of Glide Memorial Church in San Francisco, California, said it best: "Knowing and loving God is about knowing and loving yourself."

The art of knowing and loving one's self is not just about self-esteem. It's also based in spirituality. Spirituality means "relating to sacred matters." Life is sacred; therefore, all that lives is spiritual. Spirituality as a practice is much more inclusive than traditional religious practices because it allows us to be close to ourselves and to God without the worry or tight-fitting rules that surround religion. Spirituality allows us the benefit of knowing God as a woman, child, or man because it allows us to see God in our own images. An imposed system of hierarchy is not needed in spirituality because God is as close as our faces.

Traditional religious practices have always been and will always be an important part of many of our lives because they offer a deep sense of personal fellowship. However, please remember that it doesn't take religion to bring us to God. God never has and never will leave us.

As for myself, I've found that coming to a place of spirituality has allowed me to make peace with myself and God. Serving and being kind to myself is in fact serving and being kind to God in a more direct way. In the words of the noted Black poet Ntozake Shange:

> i found god in myself
> & i loved her / i loved her fiercely.

PART FOUR
▼▲▼▲▼▲▼▲▼

PUBLIC LIES
AND
PRIVATE TRUTHS

16

▼▲▼▲▼

Got a Job to Do

Careers are what white women have; jobs are
what Black women do.

—Zoey

Leave it to Zoey to break things down in simplistic
terms. Actually, girlfriend isn't too far off in her view of
things. I know, because twice a month I have this recurring fantasy that goes like this: I was born rich, and somewhere there is a secret document that proclaims me
Queen Money, but—here's the hitch—I have to find the
damn document and then my worries will be over. How's
that for magical thinking? Like I said, twice a month, the
day I pay bills and the one day a month when I desper-
ately need but can't afford to take a break from the office,
I allow myself the indulgence of the Queen Money fantasy. And then I go to work!

While I've never known my mother to work outside of
our home, she mentally prepared her six daughters to
take their places in the world. With firm sincerity, Momi
always told us, "Don't expect a knight in shiny armor to
sweep you off your feet; if anything, he'll hand you the
broom."

Economic survival is one of the hardest struggles for
Black women. In a nation where people of color are
becoming a substantial majority, our earned monthly
capital is in the minority. Throughout history and across
the nation, Black women have always outnumbered

white women in the work force, and historically, Black women have remained grossly underpaid in comparison to white women, most of whom didn't truly enter the work force until World War II.

Mama always told me that a dollar bill was a Black woman's best friend. Mama says a dollar don't give you no lip, it'll feed you when you're hungry, clothe you when you're cold, and keep the rain off your head. Yes ma'am, if you treat a dollar right, it multiplies, and if you don't it disappears, but if you got a dollar, you've got a friend for life.

—Flo

Having a dollar isn't always the problem. The problem is having enough dollars to sustain a reasonable standard of living. On the surface, it appears that as a race our overall economic standing has improved, but in reality our earning power has remained consistently low. Affirmative action and the women's movement offered us the illusion of inclusion in the job market by allowing us to move through a few corporate doors instead of kitchen doors. However, the highly visible positions of receptionist, secretary, and office clerk are often the lowest-paying positions and rarely are stepping stones for advancement.

I've been in the same position at the post office for fourteen years. I work my butt off trying to get ahead, but every time I apply for an upgrade in position, there is always some half-assed excuse or reason not to promote me.

—Flo

I know what you're saying. I trained the man my supervisor brought into our company last year. I should have gotten that position. When I filed a grievance, I was told the company needed new blood in order to put a fresh perspective on things. What really burns me up is even with my next raise I still won't match the new guy's entry-level salary. Hell, I need new money to help my perspective on living, but who can afford to quit?

—Della

We all know that discrimination is alive and well, showing its ugly presence in the form of pitiful excuses that keep us locked into low-paying, backbreaking positions. Quitting is always an option, but it's certainly not very realistic when our daily survival depends on our paychecks.

Looking for another job requires time, planning, and energy, three essential elements that are always in short supply in our lives. Juggling job, family, and home responsibilities isn't a new concept for us—we've developed this concept to an art form. Over the years media hype would have us believe that women have elevated their positions and earning power considerably because of the women's movement. Unfortunately, the media's image is clearly out of focus, targeting only a very small percentage of women, most of whom are white and middle class.

Every time I go into a production meeting at work I feel like I have to fire up a blowtorch, while everybody else strikes a match. I'm tired of always having to do more, for the same amount, just to prove I'm as bright as they are.

—Vy

The women's movement offered the promise of equality, but when the smoke from the battle cleared, we once again found ourselves out in the open field, shouldering more responsibility without the benefit of compensation for services rendered. Prior experience of discrimination and exploitation in the real, cold world has been a strict and demanding teacher, and we have been loyal, attentive students. We've learned that being given impressive titles and lofty positions without adequate wages is analogous to being handed a china plate that's been licked clean.

Frankly, I'm tired of my job, but I'm going to be there for a while, 'cause a closed mouth don't get fed, and I don't like being hungry. So how do I get to feel better about myself and not go hungry at the same time?
—*Flo*

In a society that values what you do (male concept) over who you are (female concept), it has been difficult for us as Black women to gain ground. In the employment world of males, value is placed on competition for the dollar: "I worked harder; therefore, I'm worth more." In the employment world of females, value is placed more on titles: "I'm executive director of social health; therefore, I deserve more respect." It's become increasingly difficult to feel good about ourselves in employment positions that deny us earning power or respect. As master survivalists, we've learned the practical art of shielding our pride by masking our thoughts and feelings concerning the injustices we encounter in our work situations. We turn our hurt, frustration, and anger inward and seduce ourselves and others into believing we're strong.

I've got an important secret to share, girlfriend. The reality of being strong means that we always know what our options are and when to put those options to work for ourselves. Having options is like having money in the bank, and we get to make a withdrawal whenever we please. However, before we can get a clear view of our options, we have to do one thing: we have to release ourselves from the belief that we are the job we do. We are not our job. Yes, I know it's easier said than done. But think about it for a moment. The given facts of life show that we're Black and we're women but most of all we're human. Having options and feeling good about ourselves aren't dependent on titles, positions, or money. Sure, these things help us to survive, but so does breathing.

> *Feeling good about myself doesn't pay my rent, and unless Ben Franklin's picture is grinning at me from the front of these options, I can't see how they'll be helpful.*
> —*Della*

Della's right. Feeling good about yourself doesn't pay the rent, but feeling good about yourself does translate into having more emotional energy, which you'll need to get a clearer picture of your options. Feeling good about yourself bolsters your self-confidence and emotional energy. When you have more energy, you can do things like take additional classes or workshops to increase your knowledge and skills, which in turn may lead to better employment opportunities. Having more energy might lead to opening your own business or developing a talent into a part-time job option.

The formula looks like this, sis: **Feeling good about you = emotional energy = options = physical strength = taking some form of action.**

> *How can I get emotional energy when my supervisor is always at my throat? No matter what I do, this woman has a complaint.*
>
> —*Jean*

Let's face it, sometimes we're going to deal with difficult supervisors and coworkers. Some people are just not going to be pleased. If we're doing our best, that's what counts. Again, the bottom line is we are not the job. Feeling good about ourselves depends in part on our doing the very best job we know how to do. In difficult situations, we can boost our emotional energy as a means of dealing with the stress. Some of the sisters from my sister circle volunteered a few energy boosters that have worked for them in stressful situations:

Ways to Raise Your Emotional Energy Level

1. Stash enough money from your paycheck to take yourself to lunch once a week.
2. Take flowers to work.
3. Wear something new, even if it's only nail polish, every week.
4. Listen to your favorite tunes on the way to work every day.
5. Plan something special for yourself after work each day, like a movie, window shopping, a good dinner, and the like.
6. Write down your favorite quote or Bible scripture on a slip of paper and read it during stressful times.
7. Exercise after work.
8. Take part in activities or organizations away from work that increase your sense of self empowerment, e.g., church, community groups, local women's groups.
9. For sisters who don't share their work environment with other Black women, network with other sisters in the community.
10. Take a class.
11. Explore your hobbies, talents, and skills for possible marketing potential.

Some of these suggestions might fit your needs, or there may be others that work better for you. The important thing to remember is to do something that allows you to feel good about yourself. Remember, we can't always depend on our jobs to give us the power we need to feel good about ourselves. So the key is to empower ourselves by taking actions that increase our personal self-worth on or off the job.

17

▼▲▼▲▼

Up Close and Personal

What ya look'n at, bitch?

—One young sister confronting another at a bus stop

Girlfriend! Girlfriend! Girlfriend! Something needs to be said, said, said. I'm talk'n now, right this minute, do you hear me? This kind of mess between sisters has got to go. We've got to put the word out, this trash has got to stop now!

—Zoey

Leave it to Zoey to get her meaning across in clear, direct terms. But girlfriend has made a serious point—when we trash each other, we're trashing ourselves.

Well, it's not hard to understand why this kind of thing is go'n on. We don't have any role models to look up to. Everywhere we turn folks is put'n us down, music, television, everywhere. One sister even had the nerve to write a book that says we're dirty, nasty, and lazy, and to top it off, she even said that it's okay for our men to slap us around. Now how is hearing this mess supposed to make us feel?

—Maxie

It's true, we don't always get validation from others, even other Black women. However, not getting validation is no excuse for abusing ourselves or anybody else.

The simple truth is that when we validate another sister in a positive way, we're really validating ourselves, because we're all reflections of each other.

You best say some more about this validation thing, 'cause if somebody calls me a bitch, I'm go'n to validate the hell out 'a them with my fist.

—*Flo*

When we acknowledge another sister's presence or specialness, we're in fact telling her and ourselves that we feel good about being Black women. We're also creating a positive role model because what we're expressing is healthy self-acceptance. Hearing sisters calling each other degrading names is painful, but let's face it, a lot of young sisters and even a few older ones are hurting on a deep emotional level. They're not happy with themselves, and the problems that cause their pain make them feel vengeful toward the world, so for many of these sisters the only recourse is to lash out at other Black women. These sisters need to know that there is pride and self-worth in being a Black woman. And we're the ones to give them the message by showing a sense of caring and compassion.

I don't know about that, sis. As for myself, I don't always hold with what some of these young sisters are doing. They out there tak'n drugs, hav'n babies, and God only knows what else. Don't seem like nothing I'm go'n to say is go'n to make a difference.

—*Bess*

This is not about passing judgment or changing someone's life-style. This is about acceptance. We're not all alike even in our Blackness, so it's understandable that some sisters are going to make life choices that we wouldn't make for ourselves. However, not making the same choices doesn't make us any less Black, nor does it make us any less women. When we ignore or discount another Black woman—regardless of age, sexual orientation, or life-style—we're sending the message that she is unacceptable, and we're also giving that message to ourselves. Some sisters don't have the resources, such as employment, support systems, money, homes, and many other things that a lot of us take for granted. It hurts to be deprived or feel left out. And pain makes some people angry.

When we hear sisters calling each other names or disrespecting each other, we're witnessing an act of self-hatred. It's a pretty safe bet that these sisters have known very little love and acceptance in their personal lives. Their lack of self-acceptance feeds their fear of being unacceptable to others. This fear is powerful and can cause folks to do hurtful, dangerous things to themselves and to others.

> *I always thought that being a role model meant that you helped people to change what they were doing.*
> —Callie

Being a role model is not based on making people change their behavior. The honest truth is that no one changes unless she wants to. What we model for others is freedom of choice and self-acceptance. If all we ever see and hear about ourselves is bad, then we start believing this garbage and becoming stuck in a negative rut. By showing compassion and providing ourselves as examples, we show others that there are options and choices available to them and that we are willing to help them.

> *Maybe I'm slow, but I don't get it. How can my self-acceptance make a difference to someone else?*
> —LaTisha

When we have pride in ourselves, it shows in concrete ways. Our self-acceptance shows in the way we carry ourselves, the way we dress and speak and respond to others, the causes we believe in, and the people we care about. What we're modeling is love, love for ourselves with enough left over to share. Self-pride is a very fluid form of energy; when we have that pride, it feels natural to reach out to others with a smile or a helping hand.

> *Okay, I understand what you're saying. It's like when I donate time at the women's shelter.*
>
> *—Angie*

> *Well, I don't have the time to volunteer, but I do speak to sisters I pass on the street. Shoot! That's just good hometraining.*
>
> *—Flo*

Both of these are great examples of role modeling, acceptance, and caring. By extending ourselves in even small ways, we offer other Black women the chance to see themselves as being a part of who we are—sisters. Each and every one of us has something important we can share. Isn't it about time that we get up close and personal?

Other tangible ways of role modeling and showing self acceptance are:

- Smiling and greeting another sister when you see her on the street.
- Being supportive of other sisters by not passing judgment on their life-style choices.
- Not spreading or listening to judgmental gossip about other sisters.
- Getting involved in organizations and projects that matter to you and that contribute to the wellbeing of other sisters.

These are just a few suggestions, but it only takes doing one thing to make a difference.

18

▼▲▼▲▼

Feel'n the Feel'n

Sometimes I feel like a motherless child.

—Mahalia Jackson

Mama loved us, I know she did, but when it came to talking about or showing us how she felt, well, all I can say is, she was an empty dress. You know, she was just there.

—Vy

Showing or expressing a range of emotional feelings has always been touchy business for us as Black women. We're often described or portrayed as cold, removed, or devoid of feelings, thus giving the impression that we're somehow emotionless. Of course, the reality is we do feel. We feel deeply enough to recognize that historically it has not always been safe to share these feelings with others or even with ourselves.

Recently, my mother suffered a severe heart attack. Whenever I tried to speak of how I felt about my mother's condition to a close friend, I kept stopping in midsentence. I stopped because I couldn't get enough air to let my words out. My friend Lyn pointed out that whenever I came close to saying how I felt—terrified—I had trouble breathing. Later that evening, in discussing Momi's condition over the phone with my sister Rose, I related my earlier experience and Lyn's comment. My sister paused for a second. Then she said in a teary voice, "I'm glad you said you're afraid for Momi, 'cause now I can say I'm afraid too.'' The deep personal sense of helplessness that I heard in my sister's voice echoed throughout my body and rested in my heart. We had shared our fear in order to regain our strength.

My friend's observation and my sister's response helped me to recognize a very important fact. As a trained psychotherapist who helps others touch base with their emotional resources, I saw feelings as being very healthy. As a Black woman who grew up in a very threatening world that continually discounted people of color, I learned that showing feelings could be very unsafe. By allowing myself to express my fear, I gave myself and my sister permission to open the door and explore what once had been truly dangerous territory—feelings.

Without malice or ill intent—indeed, often with survival as a paramount goal—our parents raised us to protect ourselves by teaching us to hide the raw nakedness of our emotions behind an empty dress.

I was one of the first Black children to desegregate an all-white school in Biloxi, Mississippi. There were about five of us, between the ages of seven and ten. I remember that all of us had to meet at the church, and the Reverend, with the sisters and brothers of the church, prayed over us. And then the Reverend gave us this pep talk, about how we had to be soldiers and soldiers were brave. The whole congregation drove with us to the school, only they couldn't come in with us. I remember there were all these white people lined up across the street, and there were police cars everywhere. The white people didn't say anything, or if they did I don't remember hearing it. Anyway, they let our mothers walk us up the school steps, but they couldn't go in the school. Mama was squeezing my hand so tight until all the feeling was gone. Just before she left me, she bent down and kissed my cheek and whispered in my ear to be brave and not to let them see me cry.

Everybody was nice enough, if you call not speaking to you nice. The teacher showed me to my seat and I sat down, but I was working so hard not to cry or be scared that I didn't move from that chair all day. To this very day, and I'm forty-seven years old, no one, not the Reverend or my mama or anybody, has ever asked me if I was scared. And to this very day I can't tell you what it means to be scared 'cause being brave and being scared mean one and the same thing to me.

—Flo

We've learned to dress our emotions in the analytical cloth of denial for fear that what we feel will somehow be used against us. No one has ever told us that to feel fear, happiness, sadness, joy, or anger is a normal healthy part of being human.

It's been so long since I've thought about my feelings that I honestly don't believe I have any.

—Bess

Everybody has feelings. It's not that we don't have them, it's just that we've become experts at denying ourselves the freedom of expressing what we feel. Like anything else we ignore, when we don't express our feelings, we forget to notice them.

Healthy self-esteem requires that we acknowledge and express our emotional side.

I always thought that showing my feelings would make me seem weak and out of control, especially around white people. I was always told, don't let them know what you're think'n cause they'll do you in.

—Jo

Actually, being able to express feelings is a strength, not a weakness. Being able to express what we're feeling gives us the ability to take needed steps of action in order to move on more productively with our lives. When we ignore our feelings, they tend to keep cropping up. For instance, if you are angry at someone and don't express it, that anger may come out at the wrong target—your child or someone else you love. Or you may explode at a real inappropriate time, such as on the job.

Fear is a feeling that causes me personal difficulty. I'm not comfortable with being afraid. Actually, I don't know a whole lot of people who are at ease with fear, but as for myself, when I'm afraid, I shut down emotionally and my mind goes hog wild blowing every little thing out of proportion. When I heard my mother had a heart attack, my fear, which I tried to ignore, took over and my mind went from "Momi had a heart attack" to "Momi's dying." And honey! that one feeling which generated that catastrophic thought sent me into a live-wire tailspin. I cried for fifteen minutes with the thought that my mother was dying before I could do anything else. When I pulled myself together, I was able to call the hospital and learn that while my mother was in critical condition, she was stable and the prognosis was good. Now had I been able to recognize and deal effectively with my fear in the beginning, I could have taken the appropriate steps sooner and saved myself the energy, tears, and dread that came with the catastrophic thought that my mother was dying. I'm telling you, girlfriends, feelings are powerful, but we can only use them effectively when we recognize that we have them.

As for people being able to know what we think, the truth is no one—not our mothers, fathers, lovers, or friends—knows what we're thinking unless we share the thought with that person. In other words, if we don't tell it they don't know it. Our physical behaviors might send others signals about our thoughts, but unless we actually confirm those signals with words, the other person might be completely offbase.

My boyfriend always seems to know when I'm mad
about something, and I don't have to open my mouth.
                                        —Janet

I bet not opening your mouth is a strong signal to him
that something is not right. But unless you actually tell
him you're mad, he's only guessing—until you do open
your mouth and confirm what he suspects. For all he
knows you could have lockjaw.

Being able to know and express feelings gives us un-
limited personal power, because we become more in
touch with our own emotional needs, and we're also able
to connect better with others.

Since my mother's illness, I've started the process of
reacquainting myself with my feelings. Here are a few
things that I've done that have been helpful:

- Giving my internal sensations (feelings) a name and
  saying the name out loud, so that it becomes recognizable to me. I'm feeling nervous, I'm feeling calm,
  I'm feeling scared, and so on.
- Paying more attention to how I react when I'm in certain situations, such as in crowds, at the office, at social gatherings. What feelings surface? How do I
  handle them? Do I withdraw? Do I speak up? Does my
  stomach tighten?
- Expressing my feelings to others when I choose.
- Writing about being in different situations and de-
  scribing my feelings in great detail on paper.

As I said before, feelings are powerful. It's about time
we take off the empty dress and put on our power suits
'cause, as my son would say, we be about tak'n care of
business.

PART FIVE

▾▲▾▲▾▲▾▲▾

IN THE COMPANY OF MY SISTERS

19

▼▲▼▲▼

Sisters with a New Attitude

SHIT HAPPENS

—Bumper sticker on a rusty pickup truck

There are no accidents in the universe, and last Tuesday was no exception to this time-honored belief. I overslept. As I scrambled out of the warm nest of my waterbed, I stubbed my big toe—talk about your rude awakenings. Making a mad dash for the shower, I began countdown. With minutes ticking, I did a quick soap and rinse, polished my pearlies, saluted my crop with a dab of jeri juice, jumped into my clothes, slapped on some makeup, grabbed my briefcase, kissed the child goodbye, and raced to the car. It started right on cue. A quick glance at my watch told me that with no mishaps I could make the twenty-mile trek to my office with three minutes to spare. Yes indeedy sweetie I was in control, or so I thought as I triumphantly hummed "Born Free" and assumed my best let-the-games-begin driving posture while putting the pedal to the metal.

Now had I not been so consumed by making up for lost time, I would have noticed those juicy black clouds lurking hungrily overhead, just waiting to rain on my parade. As luck wouldn't have it, just as I reached the I-5 on-ramp, Mother Nature felt the necessary urge to pay her respects, and as the song says, "down came the rain." Now for those of you who don't live in or near the growing megatropolis of Seattle, there are only three words of warning about driving on the freeway when it rains: *Don't Do It!* As the goddess is my witness, it took me twenty minutes to get from the on-ramp to the actual freeway, so as you might have already guessed I kissed a fond farewell to those three extra minutes and mentally added an hour of make-up time to my already overcrowded schedule. Lord! My I-can-control-the-world attitude sure does hate the agony of defeat. So as I joined my fellow stationary travelers in the Seattle ritual of counting the number of raindrops that hit my windshield in five-mile increments, I noticed that I was falling into a familiar pattern of blaming myself. First I blamed myself for oversleeping, then for stubbing my toe, for getting caught in the rain, for being stuck in traffic . . . Just as I was getting to the second verse of my depressed swan song, a deteriorated pickup truck with one good taillight—hanging by a single wire— edged in front of me. And then it stalled! I almost lost my cool. I was about to roll down my window and shout obscenities at the helpless driver, when I spotted the truck's bumper sticker: SHIT HAPPENS.

This, my dear sisters, is what I call divine intervention. Those two words made me laugh so hard that I forgot all about blaming myself for the nasty mess I was in. With that laughter came the realization that shit does indeed happen. It just took a stalled pickup truck to remind me. The bumper sticker made me realize that trying to have control over situations that didn't start or end with me and blaming myself for the outcome was a major waste of personal energy.

> *Why wasn't it your fault? After all, if you had got'n up on time you might have made it to work on time. Anyway, I always thought it was my responsibility to be in control of whatever went on in my life.*
> —*Cassie*

There's a trick to being in control. Being in control of ourselves means that we have to be willing to give up control of things outside of ourselves. For instance, when I overslept I tried to make up for lost time by rushing. True, if all those other things hadn't happened, I might have been on time for work, but realistically I couldn't gain back the time, because it had already passed. When I tried to gain time, I lost perspective on just what I had control over—the present. I didn't have control of the situation, I only had control of myself in the situation.

When we feel out of control, we place a serious drain on our sense of self-esteem. By recognizing the limits of our control, we increase our self-esteem.

For example, when I saw that bumper sticker and started laughing, it dawned on me that I was blaming myself for situations that I couldn't control. When I gave up trying to be in control, I could see the humor in the situation.

> *That sounds all well and good, but how do I know when I've crossed the line of being in control of myself versus out of control of the situation.*
>
> *—Della*

A surefire indicator of not having control of a situation is excessive self-blame when things go wrong. Everybody blames themselves a little—like when you forget to pick up something at the store, or you forget to return a phone call. The problem starts when blaming yourself becomes a major theme song, as in "If only I had . . ." or "I should have . . . ," that goes on for days, weeks, months, or even years. Isn't it funny that we never give ourselves credit when things turn out okay? But honey! The minute anything screws up we're ready to nail ourselves to the first available cross. Take my being stuck in traffic. Now I have absolutely no control over how other people drive in or out of the rain. But I was more than ready to take the rap for the traffic jam. If traffic was moving along at a steady pace, I wouldn't have given it a thought. Blaming myself didn't make the traffic move any faster, it just made me feel bad.

When we choose—and it is a choice—to blame ourselves unnecessarily, the only outcome is that we're going to suffer the painful consequences of feeling bad and thinking poorly of ourselves.

But what about when other people think you should be in control of situations? Everybody tells me I should have more control over my sixteen-year-old daughter. She's skipping school and running the streets. The girl's go'n wild, but no matter what I do or say, she still doesn't mind. And then everybody blames me for how she acts 'cause I'm her mother.

—Tess

Life would be so easy if we could control other people—especially our children. But realistically we just don't have that kind of power. We want to love and protect those close to us, and because we love them it's only natural that we want to take responsibility for how they behave. But we can't control that which is outside of ourselves. Blaming ourselves for someone else's behavior doesn't really help us or them. It's the natural developmental nature of children and teenagers to act out and take risks. Throwing tantrums, talking back, and skipping school are all parts of growing up, and thus to a small degree (when these behaviors don't cause physical harm to the child or others), these behaviors fall into the normal range.

When my baby sister started using drugs, I blamed myself for a long time because I had used drugs for a while, and everybody told me she was following my example. But then I went into treatment and cleaned up my act, and she's still using. I still feel bad sometimes and think that I should have set a better example, and everybody tells me to talk to her, make her go for treatment. But Linda is twenty-five years old. I talk to her all the time, but I can't make her do anything. Any-

way, I learned through my own recovery that she's re-
sponsible for her own actions.

—Vy

Some people may try to hold us hostage about the care
and control of a loved one in the belief that they know
more about our situation than we do. If these folks offer
suggestions as to how to impose those controls, we can
choose whether to take their advice. Just remember,
when we try to control people or situations outside of ourselves the outcome is generally negative.

People always tell me I seem to have everything
under control. If they knew how out of control I am most
of the time, they would laugh.

—Jo

As Black women we've become experts at projecting
certain images, one of which is being in control. Projecting an image of control means that on some deeper level
we are in control at that time. Our feelings aren't always
facts in given situations, so it pays to check out your
thoughts, because your thoughts can distort your feelings. For example, when I thought that I could still make
it to work on time, my *thought* was "I'm in control," and
my *feeling* was joyous. When I got stopped in traffic, my
thought was "Oh damn, I'm going to be late," and my
feeling was panicky. If I hadn't thought I was in control of
the traffic jam, I might have felt mad instead of panicky.
Feeling panicky was directly linked to my thought of
being in control.

Our behavior tends to be the best indicator of our sense
of control, mainly because we don't often think about
what we're doing until after the fact.

You just lost me on that one, sis.

—Zoey

Okay, Zoey, here's an example: I tell folks I don't know how to cook, yet I cook all the time. I don't *think* about my cooking when I'm in the kitchen whipping up a big pot of gumbo. At that time I'm cooking. I only *feel* that I can't cook if the gumbo doesn't taste good, which is after I've made it. Paying close attention to our behavior (looking at what we do) will give us a better handle on our sense (what we feel) of control. No one is in complete control 100 percent of the time. The key words are *complete* and *control*, but generally this only happens if we're trying to do too many things at one time. But when we pay attention to what we do, it's safe to say we're in control of ourselves.

I know what you're say'n, sis, but sometimes it's like Black women have to have a sixth sense about stuff. Like I don't go to certain parts of the city anymore 'cause it ain't safe for Black folks. Now I've only been to that part of the city twice, but both times I got pulled over and questioned by the cops. They always let me go, but my feeling is that if I continue going over there I'm going to end up in trouble for something, and the trouble will be the color of my skin.

—Zoey

You're right, Zoey. To some degree our experiences as Black women do tend to shape our attitudes and beliefs regarding how much or how little control we have over certain situations in our lives. For example, as a race of people we've traditionally had a long history of being treated unfairly by the justice system and other government systems. That feeling, or sixth sense as it's sometimes called, is more knowledge than feeling. We've learned important facts, such as blind trust may mean certain death if we're not careful in certain situations. It's sad but true—many people still base their perceptions of us on the color of our skin. They judge us as a group even when we present ourselves as individuals. And while we can't change the way others choose to see and judge us, we can maintain our own sense of personal empowerment by knowing when we are in control.

Here are some successful hints for remaining in control:

- Stop blaming yourself. Remember the bumper sticker—SHIT HAPPENS!
- Pay close attention to how you feel when you're doing a task. What do your feelings tell you at that time?
- Give yourself the clear mental message that you are in control. It does work.

Having a sense of self-control means recognizing your own personal power. It's not hard to be sisters with a new attitude when we've got self control and self-esteem on our side.

20

▼▲▼▲▼

Mov'n On

Scars are sacred places
ancient edges
where the holy
shines through
—Charlotte Watson Sherman

"Your scars are the evidence that your wounds have healed." This was my doctor's response to my question "When will these blasted scars on my skin go away?" I was seventeen at the time and didn't really appreciate the wisdom of his answer. But as I've gotten older (and hopefully wiser), I can recognize my doctor's comment for what it truly is—a measure of hope, grounded in my ability to accept myself as a whole individual.

We all have scars. Some, like mine, are visible to the naked eye. But the majority of us carry invisible scars from the wounds of childhood abuse, dysfunctional families, broken relationships, marital disappointments, and the general sorrows of life.

Who knows, maybe if my aunt and older sisters hadn't treated me so bad when I was little, I could've had two or three degrees now and been liv'n large. Instead, here I've got two divorces and I'm slave'n my time away at a two-cent factory job just to make ends meet.

—Vy

Our physical and emotional scars are not lifetime sentences to a future of doom and gloom. As my doctor pointed out, such scars are evidence that our wounds have healed. The scars we carry are reminders that we were innocent victims and major survivors of wars over which we had no control.

> *But who's to say? If I hadn't been sexually abused as a child, I could be leading a normal life right now.*
>
> —Janet

The words *could, would, should* are reflections of a revictimizing mindset. They serve as infected bandages that we use to cover past wounds. When we say, "We could have, we should have, we would have," in reference to our past and current lives, it's the same as exchanging one soiled bandage for another soiled bandage. And soiled bandages only serve the purpose of reinfecting festering wounds. When our past wounds don't get the opportunity to heal in the proper manner, we remain victims of the hurts that caused the wounds. Our past wounds are not definitions of our present lives.

In order to have and maintain a healthy sense of self-esteem, we have to be willing to remove the soiled bandages of "could, would, and should" from our old wounds. We have to allow our wounds to form scars.

> *I don't know, sis. It sounds to me as if you think scars are something to be proud of. In my book, wounds ain't pretty, but scars ain't a whole lot better.*
>
> —Zoey

Come on, Zoey, it's like the poem at the beginning of the chapter says. Scars are sacred places, ancient places, where the holy shines through. Our scars are proof that we're survivors in the present, not victims of the past traumas we've suffered. Scars are a mark of courage—they show that we've moved on, that we've made it to the present.

Scars of any kind aren't pretty, but they are a sign that something healthy has taken place. Being survivors means that we've already done one enormously healthy thing: we've lived through the traumas that caused our wounds and produced our scars. The mere act of living means that we each have some degree of healthy self-esteem.

What about being normal? Doesn't having scars mean that we're not normal in some way?

—Jo

Having scars means that we're more than normal. Those scars mean that we're sacred. There are many people who can't cope with the physical and emotional wounds of life. They take their own lives. The very fact that we choose to live means that we value ourselves. This value is sacred, and it's a testament to personal self-esteem.

Calling someone normal is just another way of saying they're ordinary. And I am of the belief that there is nothing normal or ordinary about being a Black woman in today's world. Being a Black woman means not only that we have survived the countless physical and emotional injustices that have happened to us on a personal level, but also that we are linked to Black women who came before us. We as Black women are truly in the company of our sisters.

How can I heal when I can't forget all the things that have been done to me in the past?

—Cassie

Even though we need to heal as a group, each one of us also has to heal as an individual. Healing doesn't depend on forgetting the past. Collectively, we heal through our recognition and unity as sisters. Individually, healing is done through the act of defining yourself right now, in the present. The two most powerful words in the English language are "I am." Whenever you say "I am" in relation to yourself, you place yourself in the present. Just placing yourself in the present allows you to heal the past. Healing is a process that takes time, and learning to stay present in mind, body, and spirit will require emotional energy.

What do you mean when you say that we need to stay present?

—*Tess*

Often when we encounter stressful situations like being overwhelmed by the demands of work or never-ending home responsibilities, we mentally and emotionally retreat to past situations where we felt helpless, alone, and hurt. When we dwell on these past thoughts (the old wounds), we automatically shift the feelings of the past into our present reality. Staying present means that we give ourselves permission to look at our current situation and acknowledge the feelings we have about that situation as adult women.

For example, whenever I find myself dwelling on a past hurt or injustice, I bring myself back to the present by saying a healing affirmation. Here is one of my favorite affirmations: **I am a courageous Black woman and the Mother Spirit shines on me.**

Nothing short of long-term amnesia will make us forget our individual past history, and anything done as close as yesterday is considered history. But today is current, it's the present, and we have control over ourselves in the present. What and who we are today is not who and what we were yesterday. And what we are today is proof of our survival skills.

Sis, earlier you said somethin' about usin' affirma-
tions as part of your ritual for heal'n. Tell us some more
about that.

—Zoey

I really liked the word *ritual* that you used, Zoey, because using daily affirmations has been a ritual in my life
for years.

Affirmations are like silent prayers that we can use for
self-healing and self-empowerment. They can be used at
any time and in any situation where there is a need for
personal strength. But the most important feature of affirmations is that using them allows us to stay in the present.
We have to remember that healing takes place in the present. Here are a few that I made up that have helped me
in my healing process:

- I am in the present light of the Goddess. She will pro-
  tect and comfort me.
- I am a worthwhile person.
- I am a Black woman of dignity.

The real healing power of affirmations comes from the
power of being able to define ourselves for ourselves as
we are in the present.

I once worked with a young woman of fifteen who had
been on the streets since she was twelve. She told me
straight up that she didn't want to be in therapy, because
she liked her life just the way it was and she didn't want
to change. After reassuring her that I wouldn't try to
change her, I asked her what she liked about her life
today. In a clear, steady voice she said, "I am a working
woman, and I'm proud of it." When I asked why she was
proud of her choice, she said it was because she could
take care of herself and didn't have to ask anybody for
anything.

I never saw her again after that one appointment, but
I've thought about her often. While I didn't agree with her

life-style, I had to admire her ability to stand up and define herself, and she wasn't about to let me or anybody else take her self-definition away. I have no doubt that this young sister will survive.

When I shared this story with my friend Deborah and told her of my plan to include it in this chapter, she raised strong objections: "Surely, this can't be an example of healthy self-esteem. After all, anybody who's on the street at twelve years old didn't have a choice, and how can she feel good about that kind of life?" With sadness in her voice, she added, "She's probably dead by now of AIDS." I agree with Deborah that it's not a pretty story. And while life rarely if ever hands us as Black women pretty stories, it's not the story we're dealing with, it's how we define ourselves within the story. And this young sister's story stands out for me because she dared to challenge life by defining who she was within her story. This young sister didn't allow her past wounds to rule her current reality. While my heart goes out to her and other sisters who've shared similar lives, considering her circumstances, I believe this sister had a healthy sense of self-esteem.

Yhew! This little sis had some pretty hard knocks, but let me see if I'm catching your meaning. What I think you're say'n is that it really doesn't matter what we've done in our lives; the important thing is to remember that we all have self-esteem. Am I on track?
—Zoey

You're on track, Zoey. So often I come in contact with sisters of all ages who are ready to give up on themselves because they believe that they aren't worthy of love, acceptance, and good things in their lives. These sisters base their lack of belief in themselves on personal past histories that include guilt, shame, and other types of hurts that they've encountered. They want to give up because they don't fit a stereotype of what they think Black women should be. My message is that self-esteem isn't based on pretty pictures, stereotypes, or other people's ideas about Black women. Self-esteem is based on being who we are and our ability to define who we are as Black women, today. I loved the young sister's spirit; she was willing to fight to be herself in the world. And for her the world had to be a hard, cold, dangerous place. When Deborah said this young sister didn't have a choice regarding her life, she didn't recognize that this sister made the choice to survive in the best way that she knew how—on the streets.

I've also had the opportunity to work with another sister, who was worried that she lacked self-esteem because of her abusive past. Like many of us, this sister was fairly well established in her community and church. From all outward appearances, she seemed to have it "all together." She shared with me her tramatic childhood history of physical abuse by an aunt who took care of her when her mother died. "I buried myself in my books, because when I was quiet my aunt wouldn't mess with me." I listened quietly as the sister shared the details of her painful upbringing. When I asked how she had managed to survive the childhood abuse, she tearfully stated, "Well, I had a teacher who really liked me, and I would stay after school and help her in the classroom. Nothing big, clapping erasers, washing the blackboard, and things like that. Anyway, one day I asked her how she got to be a teacher, and she told me that she had to study real hard. Well, right then and there, I decided to be a teacher when I grew up. So I studied real hard and I was able to get a full scholarship when I finished high school, so I went to college. I used to get some of the worst beatings for coming home late from school, because my aunt didn't believe me when I told her I was with my teacher. But you know what—I didn't really care about the beatings, because I knew I was going to be a teacher. And I just kept telling myself I'm going to make it, I'm going to make it."

This sister, like the young woman in the previous story,

made the decision to survive based on her ability to define herself for herself. These women's stories, like ours, are different, but their determination is clear—survival.

As Black women, we know that life's choices don't always have a name or face. We know firsthand that shit happens sometimes just because we're who we are— Black women. So often the decisions in our lives have to be made between a bad choice and a worse choice. But the important thing is that we choose to survive. Our choices may not always fit with the ideals of mainstream society, but that doesn't have to mean that we give up believing in ourselves.

As I've said before, achieving healthy self-esteem depends on being able to define ourselves for ourselves in the present. We are not our wounds of the past, and if we allow our wounds to define our present lives, we forfeit the opportunity to live our lives in the here and now. Healthy self-esteem is a present reality, and we can have that reality with two small, very powerful words: "I am." These two words won't erase the past, but they will let the holy present shine through.

Suggested Reading

Selected list of books that our group found inspiring:

Beloved, Toni Morrison, New York: Plume, 1988

Sula, Toni Morrison, New York: Plume, 1987

The Color Purple, Alice Walker, New York: Pocket Books, 1990

Sister Outsider, Essays and Speeches, Audre Lorde, Freedom, CA: The Crossing Press, 1984

And Do Remember Me, Marita Golden, New York: Doubleday, 1992

Waiting to Exhale, Terry McMillan, New York: Viking, 1992

The Heart of a Woman, Maya Angelou, New York: Bantam, 1984

At the Bottom of the River, Jamaica Kincaid, New York: Plume, 1992

The Black Woman: An Anthology, Toni Cade, New York: Mentor, 1970

The Women of Brewster Place, Gloria Naylor, New York: Viking Penguin, 1983